The Ultimate Guide for

Stock Investing

in the Age of Negative Yields

The essential knowledge for seeking returns in different stock markets.

Taking you to the commanding heights of the financial market. Understanding the silent language among professional investors.

Alpha Wong

To Cherry, with all my love
To my parents

To my teacher
Mr. Market
who teach me the truth of how the market works
by punishing me hardly

Stock Market is an ecosystem that is always changing. The aim of all financial publications is for finding out the truth of how the market works

However,

The Truth of the market is not based on any books or any theories. The truth is inside the market.

Therefore, every time when the market is changed, we may need to review all the old rules

We are not able to change the market.
We can adapt to the changes.

Disclaimer

All the content of this book is for informational purposes only. It is very important for any investor to do your own research before making any investment. All the content in this book is not for the purpose of making investment decisions.

Contents

Preface (P. 11)

Quick Start Guide

Chapter 1 – Quick Start Guide (P.16)

The Quick Start Guide for Stock investment

Understand the stock market

Chapter 2 - Understand the Stock Market (P.22)

Why investing in the stock market?

Why does simple ETF investment may generate a good return in the long run?

Earning the Market Return (Beta)

The principle behind the stock index investing method

Short-term trading is a zero-sum game

Join the winner's game

The go-go years the 1950s to late 1960s

The late 1960s to 1970s – The stock market was dead?

1980-2000 The Golden Age for stocks

2000-2007 The years before the financial crisis

2008 Global Financial Crisis

2009-2018 The age of Quantitative Easing

Since 2018 - The age of Negative Yields

Factors affecting the long-term performance of a stock market

Beware of market Bubbles

Chapter 3 - The Tools for Stock Investment (P.48)

Stock Indexing Investment

The ETFs for US market

The ETFs for other developed markets

The ETFs for Emerging markets

The Art of Investing

Chapter 4 - The Art of Investing in different markets (P.61)

The art of investing for different markets

The art of investing in emerging markets

The case of India

The case of China

The case of resource-based markets

Concerns about exchange rate fluctuations

The Art for trading in a declining or steady market

Knowledge for Stock Analysis

Chapter 5 – Determinants of stock price (P.73)

The Art for individual Stocks Analysis

What is stock?

Why do we need a stock market?

Stock market and the economy

Who determines the stock price?

Demand-side factors

Supply Side factors

Price Mechanism of the Stock Market

The breakdown of investment return

Chapter 6 - Company Analysis (P.87)

Look inside a company's business operation

Analysis of the Revenue Growth

Cost of Production Analysis

Profit Growth Analysis

Understanding the ROE

Understanding the ROA

Understand the P/E Ratio

Understand EPS growth

Balance Sheet Analysis

Debt level Analysis

Cash Flow Analysis

Chapter 7 - Stock Momentum (P.104)

About the Momentum Factor

Trade Volume (Liquidity)

Price Trend

Price Reference point: Support / Resistance

Breakthrough

Moving average

RSI

MACD

Limitations of Momentum factor analysis

Seeking for Excess Return

Chapter 8 - Capture the Alpha (P.118)

The Art of security analysis

Traditional valuation tools for a Stock portfolio

Competitive Value Viewpoint

Don't rely on any stock pricing Model

Core factor and Noise factor

Ignore the noise, learn how to capture the Alpha

Market / Stock Selection

Market Timing

Capture for the Momentum

Events Bonus

Reform Bonus

Monetary Bonus

Size of the portfolio and investment performance

Rational ignorance – Only aim for the market return

Chapter 9 - The Bango Stocks (P.140)

The case of Apple (AAPL)

The case of Tencent (TCEHY)

Returns come from changing business model

Some Important Ideas

Chapter 10 - Important Investment Ideas (P.144)

Understand the compound interest effects

Beware of Financial Fakery

A good company can be a bad investment

Understand the nature of asset price bubbles

Understand the VIX Index and implied volatility.

Using Stock options as insurance for a stock portfolio

The Age of Negative Yields

Chapter 11 - The Age of Negative Yields (P.157)

The Age of Negative Yields

What are the meanings of negative yields?

Understand our monetary system

The logic behind the monetary policy

The different types of monetary policies

Inequality will become a big problem

An Investor better be a good thinker

What can we do as an individual investor?

How to find positive returns in a distorted market.

Know yourself before investing

Chapter 12 - Know yourself (P.187)

Why do you invest?

What is your character?

An Anxiety investor

An Impatience investor

Heartbreak trader

Chapter 13 - Checklist before investing (P.193)

Do you have long-term capital?

How much you can lose?

Short term trading or Invest for the long run?

Do you have plans before investing?

Do you know the market and yourself?

Afterword (P.202)

Appendix: (P.207)

Recommended Readings

Preface

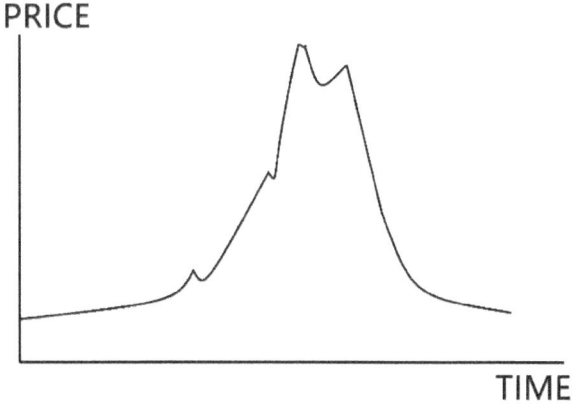

Do you know the above pattern can refer to which market event? The UK South Sea Bubble in the 1720s? The US Dot-Com Bubble in the Year 2000? The China A-Share Bubble in the year 2007? The diagram can refer to all of them! History always repeats itself, especially for the financial market. Obviously, learning can add value to a stock investor to avoid some mistakes.

This book is writing for all individual investors and people who are interested in stock investments. This little book will help you to catch up with some most important principles of stock investment in one day. I used more than ten years to accumulate all this knowledge, reading hundreds of investment books with extensive trading in different markets, both developed countries and emerging markets.

The purpose of this book is simple, increase your profitability by building up your knowledge and investing senses in the market. I will try to make everything simple and easy to understand, even you don't have any academic background, you find this book is easy to read. It's like someone is talking with you, sharing about his experience and let you think about some ideas by yourself.

Try an error may be costless for some skills learning, but if you adopt try an error method to learn how to invest in the stock market. You may lose years of saving by a single failure. Therefore, understanding how the market works is very important. Investment knowledge may also help to improve the long-term performance of pension account by some simple portfolio changes.

I understand that learning for investment is quite boring. Many classical investment books are favor for professional investors, but they may not be suitable for the general public. I also understand that most readers don't favor long writings. The most common reading device is our mobile phone. I will try to make this book 's content suitable for you to read in any device. Therefore, you can use your boring travelling time to learn something valuable. I will help you to find out some easiest way to join the stock market.

Investors can know how to start their investment after the first 10mins of reading of this book with the quick start guide. I don't want to write many long stories that wasting for reader's time. The ideas in this book will be straight forward with some necessary examples and illustrations.

In the following chapters, I will tell you why simple investment methods can earning for good market returns in some markets. You will also learn why it doesn't work in other markets. This kind of practice knowledge is from real market observations. My teacher is called Mr. Market! The best knowledge of investment is inside the market, and I will try to abstract some knowledge to you from my teacher.

There are some main questions I would like to answer in this book:

- How to trade?

- What are the determinants of the stock price?

- Why some markets always going up, but some markets only have fluctuations without long-term growth?

- How to protect our maximum loss

- How to earn the market return (Beta)?

- Are there any ways that can help-seeking for the Alpha?

Alpha refers to the excess return of an asset that outperforms the average performance of the asset class with the same level of risk. One big incentive for investment learning is to seeking Alpha return. Otherwise, we can easily obtain the Market return (Beta) by holding some simple investment tools. I will teach you some simple steps to obtain the market return within 10 minutes. I will also explain some possible ways (without guarantee) to earn the Extra return (Alpha) return in the later Chapters. You will have a better understanding of how the stock market works.

In the later part of this book, I will analyze the impact of negative yields on the stock market. The stocks market's ecosystem may have some big changes during the age of negative yields. This book may be one of the first books which discussing about the impact of negative yields. Negative yields are like an anti-gravity factor for the stock market. The market can go down due to recession but eventually will move back to a trading range which has a higher valuation level than before. Too much money is tracing too little real assets! I will also discuss the central banks' different monetary policies tools and its side effects on the financial world.

Making mistakes is unavoidable for most of the investors. Learning can help to reduce the chance of having a mistake, especially avoid some serious failure due to overconfidence. Investing in stocks is very simple, which can be described as a buy and sell order in the stock market. The market 's door always opens for everyone, whether you understand how it works will affect your profits in the long run. Let 's starts our learning journey.

Quick Start Guide

The Quick Start Guide for Stock investment

Investing in the stock market is very simple. In the first step, you need to open an investment account that can trade for stocks. You can easily open a stock trading account via the internet. After you submitted all the required documents and deposited your money, you can start to trade.

In the next step, open the trading platform, and key in the stock code for the S&P 500 index related ETF. You can type either SPY, IVV or VOO, which are the three most popular ETF for tracing the S&P 500 index 's performance with a very similar return. Then entering the number of shares, you want to buy, place the buying order, and send out to the market for execution. You have completed your first investment.

For example, if the current market price for the S&P 500 Index ETF (SPY) is $300, the BID price is 300, the ASK price is $300.1. It means that you can immediately purchase the SPY at 300.1, or you can place a buy order for $300 (queuing) and waiting if any seller would like to sell you at $300 instead of $300.1. If you would like to buy one share, then you only need to prepare around $300 plus the commission and fees (normally within 1 dollar) in your stock account. The stock market welcomes everyone, even for those only have a little amount of capital. College students already can start their stock investment with their part-time income. After your purchase order of the S&P related ETF is submitted to the market, once your purchase order is successfully matched with sellers and completely executed. You now become a real stock investor who is holding a portfolio consisting of 500 most representative firms in the US market, including Google, Apple, Facebook, Microsoft, Netflix, Coca Cola, McDonald......

You can enjoy the market return by holding such ETF (Exchange Trade fund), it means that the single investment you are trading is an investment portfolio consisted of 500 highly selected stocks, the fund 's management expense is less than 0.1% per year which can be ignored. You do not need to obtain an academic degree in finance to learn how to diversify your investment portfolio, your stock investment already welly diversified, you only need to face the market risk instead of individual stock risk.

Even one of the stocks in the portfolio has big trouble and dropped more than 20% in one trading day, the impact on your Index fund investment most likely will be less than 1%. You can hold such ETF investing as long as you want, you do no need to look at the stock market every day. You can enjoy the long-term return from the market by just holding for it in the long run. You can enjoy the market return the same as what other professional investors are doing. Warrant Buffet 's annualized return from 2009 to 2019 is highly similar to the S&P index 's performance. That 's good enough that you can use such simple tools to obtain a similar return for professional investors. In the past 50 years, the annualized return of holding the S&P index fund is around 7% (but depends on the sampling period, some 10-year interval return was 2-3% only). If your investment horizon is more than 20 years, the return from the stock market is good enough to maintain the purchasing power of your money. Most of the investors can enjoy a real return in terms of purchasing power improvement for long-term investment.

If you worry that you are buying the stock at the peak of the market cycle, you can use a monthly regular investment method instead of a lump-sum purchase. For example, you can buy the index fund monthly using your monthly savings (as low as $100 each time). We call this investment method as a dollar-cost averaging strategy. You do not need to worry about market timing problem when the market is in the downturn. You can purchase more shares if the market price becomes lower. Buying at the downturn (smile curve) could lower your average cost of the stock portfolio, which can help you to enjoy a higher potential return in the future. This method is very simple, and the investment return is good enough for the general public to prepare for their retirement.

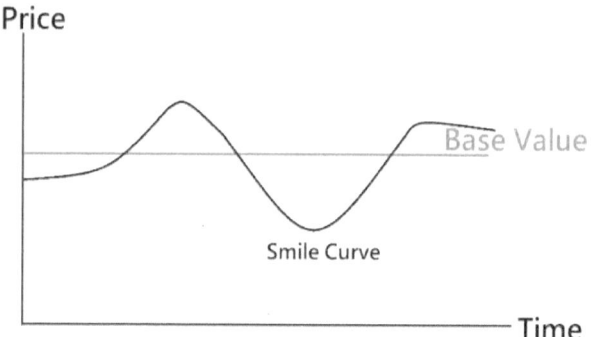

Is this investment strategy simple enough? You now know one of the simplest ways to join the market. You may be able to stop here, but obviously, the book is not that short. What I want to tell you next?

Everything seems all right for such kind of simple ETF investment strategy.   But one thing you should be cautious is that this method only works with an assumption that the S&P 500 index would keep on climbing up in the coming years. If the next 50 years' stock market performance is similar to the past 50 years, you can stop reading and just starting to build up your assets by simple monthly investing.

The only thing that never changes is – everything is always changing. Investors always build up some investment ideas or even life principles based on our experience. If some method worked for more than 50 years, we believe that it will also work for the next 50 years.

We are now in an age of negative yielding which the long-term government bond yield of many countries become negative. It means that we live in a heavily distorted financial world. The past experience may not always be correct, or at least, we should be cautious that some factors may have a great impact on the long-term market performance in the future. If you want to learn more, let's start our new learning journey to understand more deeply about stock market works.

Understand the Stock Market

Why investing in the stock market?

Stock investment generates the highest return among all the major asset types, including bonds, real estate, commodities in the US in the past century. The typical consensus for long-term investment is around 7% annualized return, the actual return varies from 5 to 10% during different buying times, if you are very unlucky which buy in the peak, you will earn a positive return for any 15 years investment time horizon. The bond market only can beat the stock during some high-interest periods like the 1970s. The bond yield is as high as double-digit. The exception already happened when some years that the bond yield rate significantly decreases which pushed up the bond price in a short period.

Traditionally, buying a stock means that you become a shareholder of a company who is normally have voting rights in the shareholder 's meeting. Buying a stock market ETF means that you indirectly become a shareholder of hundreds of companies, but without voting rights in the shareholder 's meeting. Shareholder 's meeting will elect for directors and make some important decisions. Very few individual shareholders will appear in the shareholder's meeting as they only have very little voting power. Some Japanese company will provide gifts for shareholders who attend such annual meeting. Some Japanese stock investment magazines have special chapters for how an investor can buy very few shares then attend the annual meeting to earn such gifts, and this is quite popular among the retired elderly in Japan.

For most of us, we are not investing for some gifts in the shareholders' meeting. Understand the purpose of investment is very important. Do you invest in stock as your retirement fund? Are you building up personal wealth? Want to take short-term profit? What is your investment duration? Return objectives? All these factors will significantly affect your investment decisions.

Why does simple ETF investment may generate a good return in the long run?

Simple ETF investment doesn't mean for a poor return. The typical example we used as well long-term ETF investment is the S&P 500 index fund. The main reason is the US is an opened economy, and many people bring great ideas and business models to this place. The US financial market is opened for all the qualified companies all over the world to issue shares. An investor can find all kinds of companies and investment tools in the US market. Therefore, many new firms appear, and those growth stock 's shares will include in the market index. The market index can capture those financial stars in their growing stage. The stock index is continuously revising and replacing the non-competitive firms by the new energetic company.

If your own country 's stock market is small and can't affect too many competitive firms to be listed, the ideas of stock for the long run may not be appropriate.

Technological improvement is another factor that will promote long-term stock market growth, each time a new type of technical improvement appear, the new company may have IPO (Initial Public offer, means first-time issue share to the public) in the stock market, new firms have a great chance to grow with the new funding, the stock market has chance to grow with new stars. New energetic firms that include in the index may be growing very fast in terms of sales revenue. The EPS is keeping on raising. Stock Index Investor can capture lots of benefits from that kind of long-term growth. Think about the technologically related shares like Microsoft in the 1990s, the Amazon, Apple, Facebook, Google in recent years. These kinds of growing stocks contribute to the long-term growing momentum for the US Stok market.

Earning the Market Return (Beta)

Earning market return (Beta) is not a bad idea for investors. It is simple, and the return may not be bad. As we mentioned before, the long-term stock investment return is around 7% for the US market. The return is quite attractive compared with other major asset types. You can buy the S&P 500 related ETF and then can enjoy the market return with any extra knowledge is required. That's simple and good enough.

However, we must consider some drawbacks of the stock market index investment. Even investing in the US market, if you make a lump-sum purchase at some peak timing like 1987 October, the dot-com bubble in year 2000 or the boom before the financial crisis in 2007, your investment still need to suffer for certain period of time before they can become profitable again, it may take 10 years for a price recovery.

Besides, the strategy of holding the stock market index for long-term investment only works for the US market it does not always work well in other countries. If we take the Japanese market as an example, the stock index Nikkei 225 peaked at around 41900 index points in 1989, after 30 years (in 2019) the stock index Nikkei 225 traded at around 22200 index point, the index never be able to climb back to the peak level. If you look into some of Peter Lynch 's investment books which mentioned how crazy the Japanese stock market was in the late 1980s, you are very hard to imagine how it was performing in the 1990s.

Stock for the long run is not a universal principle that can apply to different stock markets. Many emerging countries have significant price fluctuation in recent decades without observable long-term growth. The economy is growing, but the shareholder's account value didn't grow together.

S&P index is one of the best stock indexes you can invest. But will the index still be the best performing major stock index in the future? Any other markets may outperform the US index with a similar risk level? These are questions that a serious investor will think.   To solve such kind of question, we should know what the logic behind stock for the long run is.

The principle behind the stock index investing method

Stock Indexing fund is a quantitative investment. The company who determine and update the index used some quantitative measure that can make sure the index already included the most important companies in the market. Therefore, you are not buying any single investment. You have purchased a quantitative portfolio which reflected the stock market performance, or some specific sector performance if you buy some industry EFT (like technological firm).

Short-term trading is a zero-sum game
If the total stock market value doesn't grow, when there are winners who can take profit from the market, there must have the same number of losers. The main point is, how can you win that kind of game and become a winner. You can't learn from any publications for how to win a zero-sum game, as every day is a new game. Old patterns and strategies don't work. It means that your technical analysis or any quantitative signal that worked in the past may not generate profits in the future.

For a zero-sum game, one trader 's gain must be another trader 's loss. In the short run, the market price trend will move in a pattern that the least investors can follow and take profit. The price is not just moving up. It is not just moving down; it will move up and down serval times that make many followers cut loose and cut loose again. Most of us can earn some profit in some of the independent games. Eventually, most of us will lose money and leave the market. The investors will disappear from the market. This phenomenon already happened in many emerging markets. Some parents will tell their child, invest in stock is like gambling, don't touch it for your life. A fewer new generation will want to learn or even pay some attention to the stock market. They will lose the opportunity of the return from the stock investment.

Join the winner 's game

Remember, stock investment is one of the highest returns major asset types in some developed countries such as the US market If you invest for a 30 years horizon. Stock investment is absolutely a winner 's game in some market. You only need to know how to join and when to take caution for some extreme conditions. Stock for the long run can benefit most of the marker player, "If" the market is rising gradually.

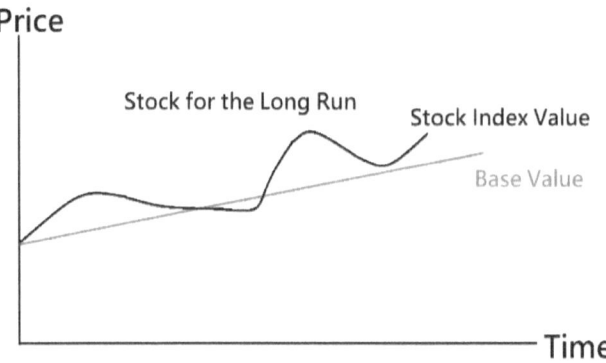

Stock for the long run may be wrong if the market raise significantly in one to two years that overdraft the future growth potential. This kind of phenomenon always happened in an emerging market, but it may happen in the developed market as well. See what happened in the year 2017. The stock market index kept on raising without major adjustments. It overdraft the growth for the coming years. In 2018 to middle 2019, the market only has adjustments, but without a significant increase in the stock price.

Join the winner's game is a good idea for most of the investors, but keep something deep inside your mind.

1) Once the market 's performance drive by short-term finance. You should be very cautious. The game will become unsustainable.

2) If the monetary background is projected to be tightening, reduce your risk assets (stocks) 's a proportion. Increase the proportion of cash or short-term money market tool. Don't switch your stocks into long-term bond investment. Both the bond market and the stock market will be significantly harmed by tightening monetary policy (interest rate unexpectedly increase), late 2018 already provided a very good lesson for all the investors. Both stock and long-term bond markets will suffer a huge loss when the market interest rate kept on raising. The performance of the market will not have a strong correlation with the economy. Even when the economy is booming, the stock market and bond market can be bad.

The Big picture of long-term market performance :
Using the US market as an example
Long-term stock growth of the U.S. market

The go-go years the 1950s to late 1960s
From 1950 to 1965, the stock market of the US was growing very fast due to the fast-economic growth of the US economy. The

stock return is quite well, and this is the golden age for value investors such as Benjamin Graham. Warren Buffet started his career in the 1950s as well.

The late 1960s to 1970s – The stock market was dead?

The stock index didn't show any growth but have serval times of downside fluctuation from 1965 to early 1980. The 1970s was a period of high-interest rates. The main reason is due to the US dollar de-linked with the gold (the end of the Bretton Woods system). US central bank needed to raise the interest rate to avoid the sharp depreciation of the US dollar. The Bond market 's yield rate was higher than 10%, and the stock market became unattractive. Besides, there wasn't any technology advance in the business world. Therefore, the stock market is underperforming with other asset classes.

1980-2000 The Golden Age for Stocks

In the 1980s, President Ronald Reagan launched certain supply-side reforms to boost the Us economy. These including tax reforms that are cutting the maximum marginal income tax rate from 70% to 50%, he also lowered the corporate tax, which encouraged more investment from the private market. Many industries also benefited from deregulations policies and became more competitive in the global market.

The central bank significantly increased the interest rate in the early 1980s successfully controlled the inflation rate. The central bank was able to lower the interest rate after the inflation rate becomes lower. As bond yields were declining, the stock market becomes relatively attractive again.

Deregulations policies in the credit market allowed the market interest rate to be more flexible, which can lower the cost of investment. This reform encouraged the growth of financial institutions, supporting the growth of venture capital, many new technology companies like Microsoft, Apple started in those ages, the profitability of the new firms supported the growth of the US market.

The lowering interest rate in 1980 was adding fuels to the stock market, and the stock market kept on rising in the middle of the 1980s. In 1987, the stock market raised almost 30% in the first nine months. The stock market had a sudden single day's crash on 19 October 1987, the major stock index lost more than 20% and leads to short chaos in the global financial market.

The most interesting thing was when many stock analysts considered the stock market would go into a new dark age, the stock market moved in the other direction. The stock market almost at its bottom level on the day of the market crash, it never comes back to such level again in the later years. The market increased by more than 300% in the coming ten years!

When the idea of the internet first introduced to the business world, it eventually leads to a new type of bubble. Many companies can raise millions of funding by simply setting up a website. They don't need any business earning, or even don't have any business models, and the valuation can base on the number of visits to the website or even based on imagination. For any zero-sum stock bubble game, what goes up must come down!

2000-2007 The years before the financial crisis
After the dot-com bubble eventually brushed in the late year 2000. The US stock market declined for two more years. The Federal Reserve lowered the interest rate tried to save the market, it works, but a new monster was growing up under such easing financial environment – subprime mortgage bubble. The property price enjoys a double-digit increase in serval years due to the flooding credits was pumping into the property market.

The stock market was growing from 2003 to 2007, and the easing monetary environment also provides hot money flow into many emerging financial markets such as China, India, Brazil, Russia.

2008 Global Financial Crisis

The lower interest rate environment eventually leads to the 2008 global financial crisis. The biggest problem is such a crisis significantly damaged the banking system 's creditability, and it leads to a credit crunch problem that banks are unable to provide credits to the public, this finally leads to serious recessions.

When the US government decided not to save for Lehman Brother in September 2018, the whole financial market was in chaos. Many financial institutions do not willing to provide finance for another as they don't know who will be collapsed next. This leaded to credit crunch problem. The US stock market dropped more than 40% value in one year or 50% from the peak from 2007. Some emerging markets lost more than 70% value in the same period.

2009-2018 The age of Quantitative Easing

To save the financial crisis, the central bank started to lower the interest rate altogether. Many of them cut short-term targeted interest from around 5% to around 0-0.5% after the crisis. But this is not enough,

many countries eventually adopted a new type of monetary policy – **quantitative easing**, which means the central bank purchases government and/or commercial bonds in the bond market to lower the long-term interest rate. The result is reducing the long-term borrowing cost. The government 's repayment ability for its debts is increasing. The global economy recovered from the financial crisis.

2018 till Now The age of Negative Yields
The Japanese government's long-term bond yields became negative in 2016, the European central bank followed the Japanese in 2018. We are now in a new age of negative yields.

The US market's interest is gradually raising since late 2015. At the end of 2018, the US central bank proposed to have a more aggressive interest raise against the potential inflation risk. The stock market significantly dropped in late 2018. To save the market also the economy, the central bank decided to hold the interest raise. Many thinkers like Alan Greenspan said he will not surprise if the U.S. will become negative yielding in the future. That 's nothing can stop the US to be negative yielding, Larry Summers stated that just one more bad recession can bring the U.S. market into the age of negative yields.

Negative yield is something happening right now in many developed countries. Some central banks already restarted the quantitative easing practice, many developed countries' 10-year government bond yield already be negative, such as Japan, Germany, and many European countries. It means that people are lending money to the government with no return, but also losing their principle. Negative Yields is one of the distorted financial condition we have ever seen in the modern financial system.

The stock market will continue to fluctuate due to economic and business factors, but the central bank may take a more active role in protecting the stock market. For some assets, like property in some region which does not have any ownership restrictions, the value can become rocket high. Some region 's property price is as high as 20-30 times of typical housing income. It means that many families are no longer able to purchase their own house if they don't receive any external finance from government or relatives. The rental return in some regions is lower than 1.5%.

When the other investment tools' (e.g. Bond) return becomes lower, it makes the stock investment more attractive. You can find that many developed countries' stocks market have a trend to increase until they move into a plateau level, something they will drop below the plateau due to short-term uncertainty, then it climbs back to the plateau. You can have a look for the 2018-2019 stock movement trend of the US market. They need a further drive to break through the plateau (higher profit level, a higher level of stock repurchase or further easing monetary conditions). We are hard to expect the stock market will collapse suddenly during an easing monetary condition. Too much money is tracing too few real business assets.

You need to understand that this is a highly distorted financial world. You cannot use your original textbook 's traditional knowledge to predict future movements. But one thing we must keep in mind, even the market can keep on the climb back to the plateau level. Can we take advantage of it if the future growth potential already being "Price-in"? You may purchase at the timing of heavy adjustments, or using monthly fixed investment, keep on buying during the stock decline, and sell them when the market backed to the plateau level. Such kind of market timing trading strategy may be able to obtain an Alpha return.

Factors affecting long-term performance of a stock market

1) Monetary background

The central bank 's monetary policy will significantly affect the performance of the stock market. If the central bank lowers the Interest rate level, the stock investment will become more attractive.

For example, if the total annual return for the stock is expected at 5%, the 10-year bond market return is 4%, the stock market will not be too attractive after considering the risk factor. However, if the central bank decides to ease the monetary policy, which makes the 10-year bond market interest to just 1.5%, the stock market will be far more attractive, the demand for the stock market will become stronger.

2) Relative Attractiveness among different assets

Stock is not a necessary item, people choose to put their money into the stock market is attracted by the potential investment returns. If the risk and return for other asset are more attractive than the stock market, the stock investment will not be a favorable choice for the public.

For some emerging countries like India and China, the property price in major cities is always raising with very little downside risk as the demand for housing in such cities is continuously rising. Then the stock market may not be the primary choice for the investors as the risk and return may not be too attractive. For the US market, the property price is relatively stable with the income and inflation level changes, the stock market 's real return is higher than the property market in the long run. Therefore, the stock market will become more attractive to investors.

3) The profitability of the companies

The profitability is an important concern when investing stocks. If the companies in a stock market can earn a higher level of profit during an economic boom, the stock market 's performance will generally be better in the long run.

Profitability also relies on the competitiveness of the company. If some company have some technological advancement that other competitor can't achieve in a certain period, the company have high barriers to entry which can earn a higher profit level than its competitors.

Investors should notice that some new business model only have high sales growth without any profit become some favorable items in the market. The main reason is such kind of company can tell a good story to the market; the investor can imagine them be the next Amazon in the future. These kinds of firms are the best item for speculation, and they are sometimes like a big zero-sum game, the valuation of the company who are continuously losing money for many years can be tens of billions of dollars. Such kind of share should never be Warren Buffet (Value Investor) 's choose.

4) The distribution policy of the companies

The companies' corporate policy will also affect the long-term price performance of the stock. If a company starts to repurchase the stocks may be able to enhance its stock performance. The stock repurchase will reduce the number of outstanding shares which will improve the earning per share level. Currently, stock repurchase is not subject to extra taxes. Therefore, it is more favorable than paying a dividend for shareholders which is subject to income tax.

For some countries with low dividend related taxes, the companies would directly pay a dividend to shareholders instead of stock repurchase. Investors can choose to use the dividend as reinvestment, and dividend reinvestment practice will create a compound interest effects which can enhance the long-term return. However, if the invested company have some sudden bad events happen can be severely harmful to your long-term return which we will discuss in the later chapters.

5) Market emotion and momentum factors
In the short run, market performance is driven by expectation and emotions. The price trend is the main factors affecting the market expectation and emotions. Many market players are adoptive nature which they believe that what is going up in the past, they will be going up in the future. During a market bubble phase, the stock market price can climb up every day, many people may know that it is a zero-sum game, but they believe that the stock price will continuously be raising in the future which they can still make a profit.

Stock market players are generally irrational players, and they are not trading shares based on some serious analysis. Instead, even many institutional investors are quite adaptive to the market price trend. They will purchase lots of bubble share during a stock market boom. Otherwise, they will underperform with their competitors.

6) Economic cycle

The stock market and economic performance do not have a strong correlation in the short-term. The US economy still in deep trouble in the year 2009, but that year is one of the best performing years among the US stock market history. If a stock market 's valuation level remains at a certain level for a long time, it's market index will be mainly reflecting its profitability level, which the market performance will have high correlations with the economic performance.

The economic cycle will affect profitability, but the main concerns of the market are the future expectations rather than the realized profit. Some traditional theory states that the stock market is a leading indicator that its performance is six to twelve months in advance of economic performance. However, due to the heavy distortion effects of the monetary policy, the relationship between economics cycle and stock market performance is significantly weakening.

The market will have a stronger correlation with the monetary policy changes than other factors such as profit level in the age of negative yields. The logic is simple, if the value of the stock is mainly built up by credits with very little distributable profit level. It is like a bread mainly made with Baking Soda, with a very little amount of flour (real profitability). Without continuously heating (new money supply), it will easily collapse.

Beware of Market Bubbles

As we mentioned before, the stock market is one of the best performing asset class that providing the highest long-term return in the U.S. The good performance is not just because the company generates good profits. Another key reason is the US stock market has a good eco-system. The market allows short-sellers and lots of different derivative tools available which help to keep the market value trading in a range that can mainly reflect the fundamental value growth.

If most of the general public all pulling their money into the market, the price of the average stock price will go to rocket high, but it also means the valuation level has overpriced. The worst case is, one generation 's people who can take away two generation 's capital growth in a short period. It means that all other followers who were buying stocks may only receive very little or even negative return after the stock market become extremely overvalued. The same story applies to the case of the 1929 stock crash.

Another famous example is the technological stock bubble or known as the Dot-com bubble in the year 2000, and many technology-related stocks lost more than 90% of its value in the following three years. Some firms may even shut down. The technology-related index used more than ten years for recovery, but for some other extremely overpriced markets, such kind of recovery never be happened.

The Japanese market climb at its highest level in 1989, the Nikkei 225 Index reached around 40000 index points. Thirty years later in 2019, the index is still at around 22000 points. Stock for the long run didn't apply to such kind of extremely overpriced market. Another extreme case was the of China A-Share market in 2007, the Shanghai stock market index climb above 6000 points in that year. In 2019, The market index is only around 3000 points. Stock for the long run is inappropriate for the above two markets.

I don't know how many decades a long-term investor can waste to take back their investment principle. At the same period, The Chinese average income and economy grew more than double, and the stock market index declined for a half. Who says that the shock market can reflect the economic performance of a country? Don't believe such kind of unexamined ideas, in so many emerging countries such as India, Russia, Brazil, Vietnam, their market value significantly fluctuated in some period, but the long-term growth is even worse than its GDP growth rate, some may become long-term negative return as well.

The story of bubbles never ended, under the age of negative bond yield, any extreme financial condition may become possible, don't believe what your old financial textbook says stock for the long run. If the market goes crazy, you should know that they are going crazy, and you should think about how to earn a profit or at least keep your assets safe. Don't reinvest your profit into the market, don't keep stock for long-term investment. Take the profit and run away, buy some real assets and enjoy your life.

That extreme financial conditional always happened in the emerging market. The stock index jumps to a rocket high in a 1 to 2-year time frame. However, what goes up must come down, especially for those bubbles which are financed by short-term capital! The index will fall and can't climb back to its previous peak for a very long period. We can't waste several decades for the possibility to claim back our investment principle. If you consider there may have inflation, you may lose 50% of purchasing power for just 2% inflation in a long period. Investing in the stock market bubble will become a losers' game, very few winners, lots of losers.

Exchange rate fluctuation is another important concern when you are investing in emerging countries. The growth rate of the India stock index is quite similar to the Nasdaq index in the US, but when you consider the currency depreciation (almost 50% deprecation since 2008), the performance will significantly underperform the US market. If you are interested in the treasure hunt in the financial markets, some emerging markets' cyclically profit potential may be attractive, but you should buy it at the right time and don't hold it forever. Stock for the long run doesn't work; at least it didn't work till now. Long-term philosophy may change over time, don't believe any investment principle before you reviewed your current market conditions. The market is always changing. The old rule may not be suitable for your ages.

The Tools for Stock Investment

Stock Indexing Investment

Stock Indexing Investment is one of convenience and highly efficient tools for an individual investor to join the market as what the quick start guide states that you can use very little money to purchase a stock portfolio with hundreds of stock market stars.

We will understand the core ideas about stock index investment in different markets. Then, we will discuss the valuation tools and the art of trading in different markets in the later chapters.

<u>Understanding major types of Stock index and ETFs</u>

The different stock market index has its character, and you can't use the same logic to apply all the markets.

<u>The ETF for US market</u>

Performance and characteristics of different Index for the US

S&P

S&P 500 is the most widely used stock market index for the US market. It consists of around 500 leading companies of the US market and reflected around 80% of the US market capitalization. Once you buy a unit of the index fund, you are buying a portfolio that can reflect the US market.

Typical investment Tools:

SPY is currently the biggest ETF in the field in terms of funds under management. After you typed the SPY symbol in your trading platform, you can check the current market price and entre how many shares you want to buy or sell during the normal trading hours.

If you trade outside normal trading hours, such as pre-market open, SPY ETF will have better liquidity in such kind of irregular trading hours.

IVV is another typical ETF that tracing the performance of the S&P 500 Index. The investment return is almost identical to SPY. The management fee for IVV and SPY is very similar. IVV's current management fee level and yield are lower than SPY. You can check before you invest.

VOO is another typical ETF that very similar to IVV.

The difference between the three ETF is simple, SPY has the best liquidity, so it is more favorable for short to medium terms traders.

Bid-Ask spread is an important cost of short-term trading, SPY 's Bid-Ask is quite narrow even in irregular timing. Therefore, it can save the investment cost for short to medium term investors and high-frequency traders. If you would like to buy and hold for a few years, you may consider the IVV or VOO depend on the expense between the two ETFs. The lower the fee, the higher the investment return in the long run.

NASDAQ

NASDAQ 100 Index consists of around 100 most representative companies listed on the Nasdaq stock exchange.

We also consider it as the technology shock index. Since 2009, this index is outperformed the Dow 30 and S&P 500 Index due to the strong growth of the companies' business and the increasing valuation level.

Investment Tool
Investors can directly purchase the ETF that tracing the index, and the typical ETF is **QQQ**. QQQ ETF has excellent liquidity and being one of the most popular tools for investing in the related index.

Dow

Dow Jones Industrial Average is one of the oldest indexes that represent the performance of around 30 companies listed in the US stock market. This index 's share sample is quite concentrated, and it cannot reflect the whole US market 's performance but a good index of tracing some biggest companies' performance.

The typical investment ETF is **DOW**; it has excellent liquidity and closely tracking the performance of the index.

The ETFs for other developed markets

Japan Stock Market

The typical market index for the Japanese stock market is **Nikkei 225**. But for most of the foreign traders, most of ETFs will be tracing the MSCI Japan Index.

The Typical Investment tool in the US stock market is **EWJ**

Investors should notice that the fluctuations of the Japanese Yen will be one of the big uncertainties when investing in Japan. Some investors would consider purchasing ETFs with currency hedge strategies, such as **DBJP** and **HEWJ**. These two ETFs will have a higher management fee, but they will hedge the risk of depreciation of the Japanese Yen.

In many cases, Japan's stock market will increase when its currency is depreciated against its trading partner. But currency depreciation will reduce the investment return when you are using USD to invest in such a market. The exchange hedged ETF will provide you with a better return when the Japanese currency depreciate. In contrast, you will lose the potential currency gain when the Japanese Yen is appreciating.

The ETFs for European Stock Markets
The European Market is not a hot investment option for most of global investors. But there are two investment themes for European countries, political changes, exchange rate change. Although the long-term growth rate for European countries is lower than in the US. But the market has many events trading opportunities. Many elections and events maybe happen, which may create some great investment opportunities.

European Stock Markets
VGK and **EZU** are two typical ETFs for investing European Market. If the US is decided to adopt a devaluation of currency policy,

European countries may become a good option as you may obtain good returns from currency gain like the years between 2003 to 2007 when the US adopted such policy, the return is even higher than directly investing in the US market.

German Stock Market

EWG is one of the actively traded ETFs for the German market. Germany is an export-oriented economy, and it will more likely be affected by the changes in trading terms with its trading partners such as the US.

UK Stock Market

The UK is a boring market without too much profit growth momentum. UK used the Pound as their currency instead of EURO. The value of Pound always fluctuating due to political events. UK market provides many opportunities for short-term events driven trading. **EWU** is one of the typical ETFs which traded in the US market.

Investors should notice that the liquidity level of those European ETFs is far lower than the US market ETF. If your investment amount is quite big, you need to consider gradually purchase them in a few days to avoid bidding up the price of ETFs above its

NAV too much. You may also consider purchasing the stocks of ETFs in such a market directly, but the transaction costs will be relatively high.

The ETFs for emerging markets
MSCI Emerging Market

MSCI Emerging Market is a stock market index that tracing the performance of different emerging market companies listed in the different stock exchanges. The index recognized as one of the leading indicators of the performance of the emerging market.

Investment Tools:
EMM or **VWO** EFT

Both are very similar ETFs which are tracing the performance of the same index. The EMM has better liquidity in different trading hours, especially for irregular trading hours. The VWO has a relatively lower management fee level.

India Stock Market

India is a hot market that attracting many investors, an economy with a high proportion of the young population, fast economic growth. The stock index is also climbing up in terms of local currency.

However, the return of holding India stock is not as attractive as you your projection. The most popular ETF for the India stock market is INDA. The index mainly consists of some I.T. related firms like Infosys, Financial firms like ICICI Bank and some tradition industrial companies like Reliance. These are the biggest firms in the India market, but not the firms with the fastest growth. If you consider the ETF, which focuses on domestic demand growth like INCO, you will find that the long-term return is far better than the INDIA. From 2012 to late 2019, the INCO increased more than 100%, but the INDA increased by less than 30%.

There are two important items we need to notice as a foreign investor.

1) Exchange rate risk

India 's Rupee is a typical emerging market currency that has an unstable value against USD. India is not an export-oriented economy, but an economy that is driven by domestic demand. However, India is a country that relied on energy import; its balance of payment has a long history of negative value which means its import value is persistently greater than its export value.

Therefore, its exchange rate will be significantly affected by oil price changes. The currency loses may up to 40% of the value for a 10-year horizon from 2008. The exchange loses will significantly reduce your return in terms of USD.

2) High Valuation level

The India market is a fast-growing market, some of the stock trade at a quite high valuation level. Using the INCO ETF as an example, the historical P/E is as high as 30 (US long-term is 14-18) or above, P/B is higher than 6 (the US long-term is around 3). If the company's growth rate is not fast enough, it is very difficult to justify such a high level of valuation.

This kind of story always appears in many other emerging markets. The economy is good, the company is good, but it can be a bad investment if the valuation is too high.

China Related Stock Market

China A-share Market

China A-Share is a market previously is a closed market that is dominated by domestic capital only as the China A-Share market joined the major stock index such as MSCI and FTSE with an open-market policy that allows more foreign capital to invest. It becomes one of the hot investment objects for global investors.

To invest in the China market, you can use the US market ETF **ASHR** to invest in the CSI 300 Index indirectly. CSI 300 is one of the most representative indexes of the China A-share market.

MSCI China Index
Many energetic Chinese firms listed in stock exchanges outside China 's A-Share market such as Alibaba, JD, Baidu, Tencent, etc. The MSCI index will capture these stocks in their portfolio, which makes the earning growth of the index is better than the traditional CSI 300 Index.

Similar to the India market, valuation is a big issue for trading the Chinese markets. The index of the A-share market sometime will be rocket high and become an absolute zero-sum game in a period such as the years 2007 and 2015. The Stock market Index peaked in 2007, which the market can't break the record till now. Some shares' price traded more than 200 years of their profit potential, the major shareholder in a company will have a very high incentive to sell most of their shares to the market. But investors are willing to take them all; shares are like the chips in the casino.

Most of the individual Chinese investors are short-term traders who focus on short-term profit opportunities. Their behavior is rational as the market can't apply stock for the long run concepts. The market will go crazy in some ages; please throw all your fundamental analysis tool kits at such time. It is meaningless, and every trader only focuses on stock momentum, someone takes huge profits, more of other sufferings.

Will this kind of phenomenon be changed after the China market is reformed, with a higher level of involvement of long-term institutional investors? The China A-share already included in the portfolio of some major investment index like MSCI and FTSE emerging countries and some other related index. We can expect some good changes may happen.

The reform will keep going on. The idea to invest in the China market is simple, buy it at a relatively low level and forgot what you are holding. No need to care about all the bad news, all the pessimistic comments. You only need to notice the market again when the stock market price news frequently appears in the media, and it signals the market is overheated.

We should notice that we are now in age with lots of private and venture capitals available. This means that any new firms with good business model will have enough financial support before they can go for IPO which be listed in the stock exchange. Therefore, that's no reason that they will sell the shares to you at a bargain price level.

Investor should be concerned about the valuation level of some newly listed company. If they are heavily overpriced, you may not be able to take advantage to hold it in the long run. When investing in such kind of emerging countries, any pricing level is possible, a company without any potential profit in the coming 3 to 5 years can be valued as 10 to 20 times of P/B. Trading suck kind of stock is playing a zero-sum game.

In the below chapters, we will have more discussion about why the emerging market 's performance significantly lower than its economic performance.

The Art of Investing in different markets

The art of investing for different markets

Trading in different market is an art, not a science. As mentioned before, trading in the US market is quite easy that you can apply stock for the long run practice. Just persistently accumulating stocks in any market timing, especially buying more during the stock market downturns, you already can earn a good return in the long run. This simple method works for the last 50 years.

It is simple, it is profitable, what else do you want. However, I must remind investors again if the US market is pushed up by the negative yields or extreme monetary conditions to an ultra-high level in the future, like what happened in the emerging market during a stock market bubble. The market will overdraft all the future growth potential for many years. The old players take a huge profit in a short raising period, and the new players become losers in the long run. Stock for the long run practice may not be working anymore in such kind of condition. We should adopt the market changes instead of insisting on some unexamined belief.

The art of investing in emerging markets

The emerging market's market capacity is relatively smaller than developed countries. Once a certain amount of new capital flows into the market, the market price may sudden become rocket high. But this kind of momentum will only be able to maintain in a short period. The market will reach a new roof. If the market can't break through the roof in a short period of timing, it can come down very fast. Many short-term foreign capitals who invested in emerging countries are hot money, they will leave the country quickly after the index doesn't have increasing momentum.

One interesting indicator in the previous observation is market breadth. It means that how many numbers of shares are increasing together with the market index. The idea is when the market is pushing up by hot money inflow, most of the shares in the index may increasing together. However, if the market index is increasing by only a few numbers of stocks' contributions, it means that the market 's overall performance is weakening. Some of the investors will consider leaving the market earlier when the market breadth becomes narrowing.

The case of India

India is an interesting market with some special character. India has a strong domestics market, a young and energetic workforce, and with the fast-economic growth rate. However, foreign investors are not easy to capture benefits from the market. You must be selective and be patient.

If you open the chart of the India ETF (INDA), you will find that its performance is underperforming the US market from 2012 to 2019. But the performance in some years is very attractive for more than 30% return in 12 months.

The typical pattern model of a jumping market is like that:

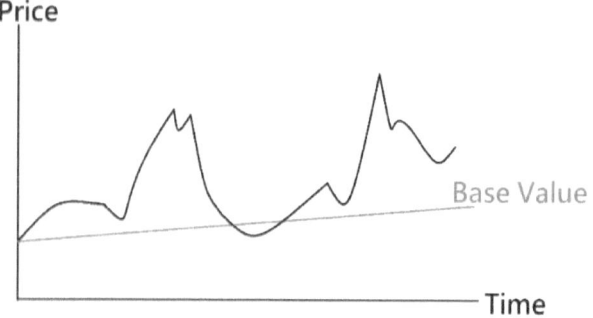

Jump-> Stay -> Fall -> Jump Again

If you want to earn an Alpha return in India market, wait and build up position during the falling stage, and then wait for another boom phase to sell off, such kind of practice can generate an extra return than buy and hold in the past. The stock market will jump again from the lower ground (close to its base value) in 3 to 5 years. The trading cycle of India share is relatively short as around 2 to 4 years. Normally investors no need to be waiting for too long for a new cycle. The India market index seems always moving up in terms of the Indian Rupee, but if you are checking the market performance in terms of USD, the market is in obvious trading in cycles. The exchange movement of Rupee is one of the important factors that will affect foreign investor's long term performance.

Another way to capture Alpha is to focus on the consumer sector of the India stock market. The relative ETF code is INCO. If you have a look at the performance of INCO and INDA, you will find that the long-term performance of INCO is significantly higher than the INDA. The INCO has more than 100% return from 2012 to third-quarter 2019. The INDA only has around a 20% return in the same period. But we should notice that the volatility of the INCO is higher than the INDA. Buying the INCO during downturn seems easier to obtain Alpha return than buying INDA at the same time because the INCO has better growth potential.

However, investors should remind that the valuation of the INCO may be at a very expensive level when the market is overheated. It may become overvalued (price in the future growth potential) when compared with other similar types of ETFs. You should keep in mind that stock for the long run doesn't work for all kinds of investment. A good performing business segment can be a bad investment if it is overpriced.

The case of China

China's stock market is another interesting market that has many similar characters with other emerging markets.

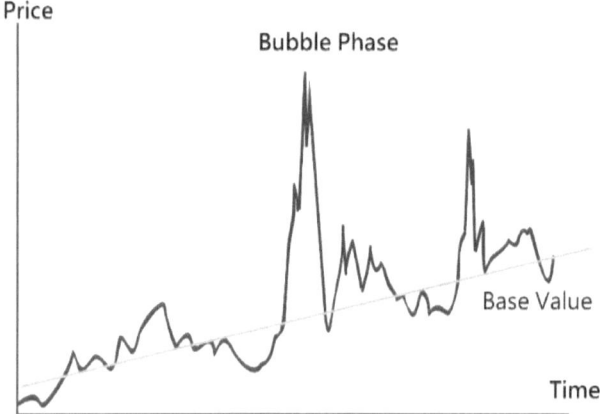

1) Highly fluctuated during a trading cycle
2) The price movement does not have a high correlation with the developed markets.
3) The stock market may stay at the bottom for a few years (1-3years), suddenly go up, most investors don't trust it at first.

However, it keeps on going up, some investors feel doubtful, and some join with it. Normally, it will have short adjustment than going up faster, investor completely believes in it. The market index goes to the highest point and then falling very quickly. The peak is normally triangle-shaped, most likely doesn't have a highland pattern before the collapse because people don't have the patience to wait.

4) Suddenly, the market falls sharply, but most of the newcomers believe that it is a stock adjustment.
5) The stock market is falling at a similar speed as it climbs up.
6) The stock market needs a few years to rebuild its confidence after one crisis.
7) The market cycle always repeats itself. The pattern is quite similar unless the market players are completely changed.

Profiting from China A share is not easy in the past. The most important thing is whether you have enough patient during the long bear market. The market will have several resistant during the period, each time the market goes down deeper after some rebound. It is very discouraging for investors seeing their investment's value is persistently decreasing. All of a sudden, no needed for any sounds reasoning, the market index quickly turns up.

Many people will be doubtful that this time is another useless rebound. But this time is different! It is going up and going up without any reason. My recommendation is don't look at the financial news when you are trading with China A-share market. The market is noise based, and fundamental factors do not have an important role in the performance of the stocks. You can't use fundamental factors to explain what happens in the market excepts you are a reporter who needs to find some "Reason". People believe that the stock market can make money is the best reason. New money is flowing into the market which creates buying pressure. This reason is simple, but such kind of changes are unpredictable. How can you know when the new investors will change their mind? Once they believe that the market can't make money any more, they will withdraw their money from the capital market. Where to find a new investor to buy their investment at such a high price?

One more important factor is many traders will borrow short-term finance to join the market, some are using stock margins which is a short-term borrowing provided by the brokerage firm. That kind of short-term finance bear high-interest costs. The collateral is the stocks in the brokerage account. If the market price can't be raising very fast, those investors who bear a high cost of borrowing already will suffer loss. This kind of short-term hot money will make the stock market more fluctuate in the final stage of the Bull market. A strong adjustment may appear at any time, many investors jump off the boat, then the stock market sharply increasing again to other new heights until they are reached the final peak. It is a casino! Don't tell me you can predict the price change in advance.

Experienced investors all know such kind of bubble market will eventually be collapsed. But when the market price is rising and rising again, people who are trying to tell others to be cautious will be considered as unsuitable old species in the new age. People do not learn from history, especially from financial history. That's why many stock markets will repeat old trading patterns again and again. If you study the price pattern in many famous speculative bubbles, you will find that they are like" Old Poison in new bottles".

The case of resources-based countries

Russia and Brazil are typical resource-based markets. These markets heavily rely on exporting primary commodities such as iron ore, agriculture products, oil, and gas. Russia 's stock market index highly correlated with the oil price, nearly half the proportion of the stock index is oil-related firms. The price of commodity increases will not just raise the stock price. The exchange rate will also be appreciated against the major currency. That's why the Russia market sometime will have excellent performance when the oil price is increasing. But the stock market will easily entre into the down cycle when the oil price is decreasing.

Oil is one of the major trading commodities. However, the future price movement of oil is very difficult to predict. In recent years, the Russia market is increasing its non-oil related sector in the economy. The correlation between oil prices and the Russia market may gradually decline in the future. Brazil has a higher proportion of basic material and energy-related firms than in emerging countries' average. Besides the financial sector, many of the Biggest Brazilian firms are mining, food processing, oil-related. Although the biggest sector in the market index is the financial sector, Brazil's stock market performance is highly correlated with the commodity price index.

Concerns about exchange rate fluctuations
Exchange rate fluctuation is one of the important concerns when

trading in emerging countries. If you look at the stock market index in terms of the local currency, you will find that the India market is increased quite fast in recent years. But when you look at the ETF traded in the US market using USD as the denomination, you will find that the performance in terms of USD is another story.

Therefore, if you are a foreign investor who can't borrow the domestic currency for investment or suing possible exchange hedging tools, we must consider the exchange risk. If the stock market index increased 100%, but the currency depreciated 50%, the investment return for a foreigner will become zero. That's why in many investment books, the author will tell the reader to put a relatively small proportion of the portfolio into the emerging market to reduce the risk exposure.

<u>The Art for trading in a declining or steady market</u>
Investors may avoid some declining market which has a population decline problem which the economy does not have long-term growth potentials, such as Japan or some European countries.

Trading such kind of market is far more difficult than those market that can apply for stock in the long run principle. However, these markets sometimes can provide you with extraordinary returns in a certain period. Why? Look at the Japanese stock market 's performance from 2012 to 2013, and you will find it outperform many developed markets. The main reason is due to "Abenomics", the Japanese prime minister Shinzo Abe adopted an aggressive monetary and fiscal policy to stimulate the economy. If you understand one of the policies is by currency depreciation and stimulate export, you purchase the exchange hedged Japanese market ETF, and the return is more than 50% in that period. 50% return in a developed market! If you ignored that kind of market, your investment opportunities would be narrowed.

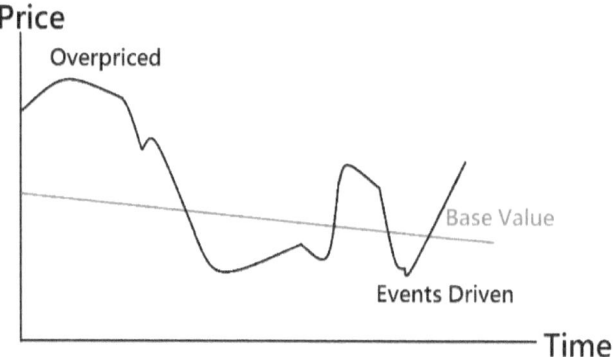

Trading in that kind of steady or declining market, which only has price fluctuations without not long-term price growth, is quite difficult and only suitable for active traders. You need to choose the right timing and keep your eyes on government policy changes (notice for those election events), both are the most important source of excess return from such kind of markets.

Determinants of Stock Price

The Art for individual Stocks Analysis

We have reviewed some core concepts about the stock market, know about some trading ideas and investment tools. Why do we still need to understand for the analysis of the individual stock?

The main point is, the market index is consisted of individual stocks, if you can understand how to analyze an individual stock, you can easier to assess a countries' stock market performance in the long run. For example, some countries like South Korea, their giant listed company is highly concentrated in a few industries. When you know how some market factors may affect the performance of these industries, you will have a better idea of how well the stock market index will perform in the future.

What is stock?

Once you brought a company's stock, you become the shareholder of the firm. You will have voting right in the shareholder 's meeting. Seldom of the individual shareholders would join the shareholder's meeting. As portfolio investment become more popular these days, many investors joining the stock market by indirect investment such as mutual funds (some ETF are mutual funds as well). They are an indirect shareholder of the company. If you look at the shareholder's list in some company, you can easily find out some investment banks' name. They are holding the shares for their clients instead of they are the final owner of these stocks.

Why do we need a stock market?

Before answering the above question, think about why we need to set up banks. Banks help to channel idle saving to investment. Besides, banks credit creation can promote long-term economic growth.

The stock market has a similar function that can channel saving or idle resources into some new business model which has good growth potential. This kind of new firm can expand and enhance the long-term economic growth of the economy.

Think about you are Bill Gates at 16 years old. You currently have a good business idea (setup competitive software company), but you don't have fixed assets as collateral to borrow money, it is very hard for him to obtain huge borrowing from banks, even the bank knows the idea most likely to be successful.

If this is a case that happened today, Bill can easily obtain millions of dollars from some venture capital. The venture capital provides funding for Bill is not just because of kindness, but the profitability of such investment. If the venture capital invested in 10 similar start-up businesses, any successful case could earn a 1000% return. It sounds a good business model. The main point is how these venture capitals can exist and get back the cash return?

When a start-up company become bigger, they may arrange for an initial public offer that issues its shares to the general public, that's very good timing for the venture capital to take profit and exit from an investment project. They can use this profit to invest in more new companies. If the stock market doesn't exist, the venture capital will be very difficult to exit from an investment. They need to find another buyer who is willing to buy their share or waiting a very long time to see whether the company can generate cash flow and start distributing profit. Obviously, this will reduce the availability of start funding, and many good business models may not have enough funding to support growth.

Stock market and the economy

The stock market is generally good for an economy for supporting business growth, but over-investment in the stock market may not be good for an economy. This will create an asset price bubble. As I mentioned before, if the stock market is a zero-sum game in some country, the stock market crash just means some people 's wealth is now in other people 's pockets. However, it is not that's not that simple in the real world.

The 1929 stock crash and 2008 global financial crisis can be so harmful to the economy are because of the credit market was involved. The bubble is built by credits, and it will severely harm the banking system when the bubble is burst. The financial institutions are not able to provide credit function to the general public, we call such kind of condition as a credit crunch. The consumer and business are very hard to obtain finance from the banking system to support their consumption and business investments. Such kind of situation is very harmful to the whole economy.

China 's A-share market tried serval timings that dropped by more than 50% in a year. But the Chinese economy still growing very fast when the stock market performed poorly in the same period. This shows that the stock market 's performance may not have too much direct impact on the real economy. It's long-term performance really depends on different countries' conditions. Whether the banking system is significantly involved in the stock market bubble is an important concern. If the banking system does not have much direct and indirect finance on the stock bubble, such kind of zero-sum game may not be too harmful to the economy. But obviously, it will be harmful to those investors who buy the stock at the peak level.

Who determines the stock price?

This simple economics concept, the stock price depends on the demand and supply-side factors changes in the market. In the real world, it is very difficult to understand what the actual demand and supply-side factors of the market are. My viewpoints are quite different from traditional textbooks.

Demand-side factors

Price Trend

The stock price increase because it is increasing. This statement is not a typo. This is a concept of investor self-reinforcement. For most of the individual investors or even mutual funds, the most attractive asset may not be the biggest share, but those share with the strongest price raising momentum. The fund managers clearly understand that they are trading with something that may not have any fundamental value or obviously overpriced items.

Refers to George Soros 's reflection theory, even people 's believe itself can change the market. When more people believed the market would be increased, they will take action and pull up the price, and the market price will really go up, the price movement will reinforce itself. When more people believe that the market will further go up, the market price increased to a new height. People 's expectation will directly change the market 's performance. If a market is increased for more than ten years, most of the people will expect the market will go up in the eleven years.

The attractiveness of the substitute

Think about the 1970s when the bond market can offer you a 10% yield, will a company offer you a 5% annual growth be attractive? That's why the stock market was underperforming in the 1970s. In contrast, when the age of negative yielding is coming, the substitutes of the stock market become less and less attractive. The stock market may have fluctuations but eventually will move back to the highland. That's the logic why Warrant Buffet says at the current interest and market condition, the stock market didn't over-priced when the US market created now record high in 2018.

If any stock crisis is coming due to recession or whatever reason, the interest rate of the US will back to zero or become negative as Alan Greenspan expected maybe happened in the future. The stock market index will go down and then raise again, yield return will become scarce resource among the investment market, people are willing to paying a high price for any asset that can generate positive yield during such kind of extreme market conditions.

Stock repurchase (Driven by the availability of capital)
The firm will use its available capital to purchase shares in the market.

Long-term inflow from Pension Fund
Long-term stable buyer, the investor seldom switching their portfolio.

Short-term Hot money (Driven by noise factors)
Hedge fund plays an active role, also private equity and many individual market players. They will follow the trend and provide liquidity. Sometimes they will accelerate the increasing rate of the stock price.

The Central Bank as a market Player

The Bank of Japan already started to purchase Japanese ETFs and becomes one of the players in the stock market. In our traditional viewpoint, a buyer of the stock will become the potential seller in the market. However, the central bank can be a permanent buyer which do not need to sell their portfolio during any kind of economic conditions. They are like a permanent buyer that will not increase the potential selling pressure, but they will reduce the stocks available for trading in the market, less individual investors can benefit from stock market improve if a higher proportion of shared is now holding in the central bank 's hand.

The role of a central bank in the stock market has its maximum limits as the number of shares available for purchase is relatively stable. If the central purchased more than 50% of the proportion of the outstanding of share, the central bank will become the market itself. The stock market will dominate by the central bank 's visible hand intervention and all the price mechanism will be distorted.

One more thing investor need to notice is not all kind of shares will be benefited from such kind of purchase. The central bank mainly will affect those company which are included in the major stock index. Those small firms outside the stock index will not have a direct benefit from such kind of investment.

Supply Side factors
Any factors that lead to selling of share will consider as a supply-side factor in the stock market

Profit Taking by investor
Some investors will quit their position and take profit after the stock price raised to a certain level. That kind of normal selling behavior sometime will lead to technical adjustments when the stock price is going up. After the stocks are sold to some investors with stronger expectations, the stock price will go up again, until they can't find anyone else has a higher expectation of the stock price, then, the stock price will start to fall.

Cutting loss
Many people will choose to cut losses if the price of their stock dropped to a certain level. A cutting loss will increase the supply of shares after the stock price dropped below a specific price point (supporting point).

Some quantitative trading programs may even try to trigger the cut loss behavior by lowering the market price by selling their own shares to a certain level. They will become a net buyer after the stock price is dropped below its target, this is a kind of favor strategy used in the zero-sum game. Short-term trading in some individual shares become more and more difficult nowadays.

Forced Selling

Some investor may borrow money for investing, If the price of the stocks is dropping at a certain level, the value of the portfolio of a leveraged investor may not be able to meet with the borrowing requirement (also known as maintenance margin). The institution that lets you the money will be able to sell some or all your portfolio. This kind of forced selling sometime may lead to an intraday crash (dropped more than 30% in one day) if a major shareholder's share is dumping into the market. Source of funding of the market players is an important supply-side consideration.

Balancing the portfolio

Mutual funds and other institutional investors will balance their portfolio in a certain period. Some of them may sell some proportion of stocks if the market goes up very fast, some investors will sell some of the stock to maintain the risk exposure in the stock market meet with their investment policy. This kind of rebalancing behavior will increase the supply of stock in the market.

The companies issuing New Stocks

Listed companies may issue additional shares during a bull market in order to obtain more working capital or financing their investment. Sometime the stock market may issue shares during the bear market if they need some immediate cash injection to finance for the company's operation.

Issue more shares are neutral to the stock price depend on the natural. If the company uses the funding for expanding the business, the stock price may go up. If they need operating cash flow, the stock price most likely will go down, the new shares will dilute their voting right and interest of the company.

Price Mechanism of the Stock Market

The price mechanism in the Stock Market is quite simple:
1) The demand for the stock is higher than the supply in a period. The stock price will go up.

2) The demand for the stock is less than the supply. The stock price will go down.

When you are quoting the stock price from your trading platform, most like you will find the bid price and ask price. Bid price refers to the price that the buyer wanted to an immediate purchase, ask price means the selling price the seller is willing to sell you instantly

See the below example for a company called The Super Alpha Co.

Bid Price	Ask Price
11.3 x 5 (Hundred)	11.5 x 3(Hundred)

If you would like to purchase 200 shares immediately, you can place your order at 11.5 (Ask price). You order most likely will be done immediately unless there are some high-frequency trader involved in your trade or the market sudden changed the price.

If you place your order at 11.3, you are now queuing at 11.3, your order may not be executed unless someone who is willing to sell you at 11.3.

The breakdown of investment return

Direct Cash Return from holding stock

1) Stock Dividend, which can be used for reinvestment

   The U.S. investors do not like a firm that pays out high dividend level as dividend are subject to income tax. The dividend yield rate is normally lower than 2% for most of the big corporations.

Capital Gain (/Loss) when you sold your shares

2) The stock repurchase is a very popular practice for U.S. corporations.

Stock repurchase can boost the EPS (Earning per share), which can support the share price as the company buys back its shares in the stock market. This can benefit its shareholders without any tax expense.

Valuation change sometimes can significantly affect the capital gain level. Valuation changes mainly due to various reasoning, such as lower interest rate, many new investors joined the stock market which pulls up the stock price level. Sometimes, the stock price is increasing already be the best reason for why the stock price is increasing. As people are likely to join any asset market when its price is going up, this is our human instinct, and people will simply imitate other people 's investing behavior in order to earn the same return. They will not think rationally that whether the market condition already changes. That's why the uptrend can be self-reinforced in many markets.

Company Analysis

Look inside a company's business operation

Business growth is a fundamental factor to support the long-term return of stock investment

Long-term dividend and valuation change heavily depend on business growth and profitability changes. These are the most important factors that contribute to investor's profit in the long run. A stock market cannot substantially generate long-term return for investors by valuation change only. When we look at a Micro level of how well a company is performing, we can have some brief understanding of the below analysis frameworks.

We can think about the business model of the firm and think about how it generates profit. For example, you can think about if any new competitors can easily appear and capture the firm profits. For most of the individual investors like you and me, we don't have time to do in-depth analysis for thousands of shares, and it's just wasting our time but may not generate any extra return. But if you want to have a better understanding of how to analyze a company, this kind of knowledge still are valuable for your portfolio investment.

Below is an example of a simplified income statement:

Simplified income statement (US$ in Million)	
Revenue	$100
Cost of Goods Sold	$60
Gross Profit	$40 ($100-$60)
Indirect Cost (administrative cost, cost of finance, depreciation) + Minor shareholder's interest, etc.	$30
Net Profit	=$10 ($40-$30)
Profit Tax	=$2
Net Profit after Tax	=$8 ($40-$30)

Most of the investor will mainly focus on revenue and net profit.

Analysis of the Revenue Growth

When we look at the financial report of a company, you can easily find the income statement item. The first item in the income statement will be Revenue item.

Revenue is the same as sales or turnover. Revenue is one of the most important items to analyze the performance of a firm. Higher sales revenue growth means a higher potential to become bigger and more profitable in the future. Therefore, a company with a higher revenue growth rate would normally enjoy a higher valuation level than a company without sales growth. The market will label such kind of stocks as growth stocks.

If a company only has a limited sized business in a market without any growth potential, you are very difficult to expect the stock price would have too much future growth potential as well. This kind of company will not be able to attract active investors unless they are selling at a bargain price.

For some fast-growing online retail companies, we may use **Sales Per Share** to assess the performance of a growth stock, the formula as below:

$$\frac{\text{Total Sales Revenue}}{\text{The average number of shares}}$$

If the sales per share of a company are growing at 25% or above, it will generally be classified as growing stock. But whether the stock price will rise, or decrease may depend on the difference between actual growth level and the expected growth level.

For example,

Actual growth rate > Expected growth rate, generally considered as positive factors to the stock price

Actual growth rate < Expected growth rate, generally considered as negative factors to the stock price

If the market consensus for a stock's sales growth per share is 30%, the company only had a 20% growth in the current period, and the management expected the growth in the future financial period will be around 20% only. It will generally consider as negative factors for the stock investors, many of them may consider selling off some of their stock holdings.

When we look inside the sales growth, one interesting idea is whether the sales growth accompanies by sales quantity increases. Some firms have a very strong brand name that can keep on raising its per-unit price level (e.g. mobile phone industry) but the sales quantity didn't growth. The investors will generally more appreciate sales quantity growth instead of sales growth driven by the per-unit price increase only. Because the firms may lose its market share and power if their sales quantity didn't growth.

The price of a non-necessity product will have its pricing limits. If you keep on raising the price level, you will lose some customers and will give your potential competitor a bigger market share. Eventually, the dominating firm may lose its market shares and market power with such kind of pricing strategy. Therefore, a sales growth driven with both sales quantity and market share increase is more favorable for investors.

Cost of Production Analysis

When we look at the company's cost structure, we better identify what the necessary cost of business and their proportion to the company's total cost are.

A higher proportion of the fixed cost (cost do not vary with output level) means that the company is more vulnerable to external shock. For example, if the rental cost is one of the main costs of a retail firm, but the firms' business location is not able to relocate as they will lose many customers. The firms do not have too much flexibility to handle raising rental cost problem.

The airline company is a typical example of a vulnerable business. Energy is one of the dominating costs when operating an airline, the rental cost of the financial cost of obtaining an aircraft is fixed cost. Once the demand for travel decreases or the oil price significantly increases, the airline company may suffer huge and record loss in the financial year. Therefore, profitability is not stable for those firms with an inflexible cost structure.

In contrast, some firms can enjoy cost advantage by the economies of scale effects. For example, a power supply company can enjoy lower average fixed costs if their service can cover with more households.

Another more debatable examples are internet service or content providers. Think about your paid online media platform like Netflix, they can provide you high-quality multimedia content at a reasonable cost, as they can share the cost of obtaining the broadcast rights of different media or film to tens of millions of clients. If any new competitor wants to join the market, they will become unprofitable if they set the same price level with Netflix, this is because they may not have enough clients to share the cost.

Natural monopoly refers to a condition that only one firm in the industry may be more beneficiary for consumers, as they can provide service at a lower price level. The additional cost of serving one more client is almost zero, more clients, more profitable. This kind of business model has a high barrier to entry, you can find the industry giant remain strong in the long run unless a super competitor with strong support from the capital market appears to compete. Now you may know why Amazon and Alibaba be so successful in the online selling field but without strong competitors that can really threaten them. Winners take it all is a typical internet business 's phenomena.

Firms with high fixed costs may not be a good business, a higher proportion of the variable cost will be more flexible. However, some infrastructure-related industries such as train service or highways, the company built the facilities long years before, the construction costs already significantly raise today. The existing form only needs to put a few levels of resources in maintaining the business. Any new competitors will face a very high fixed cost which they will not be able to survive if they charge the same price level as the existing company. The existing company can enjoy a cost advantage as barriers to entry.

Some companies have significant cost advantage if their additional cost to provide service for one more extra client is zero (Marginal cost equal zero). Such as many internet content providers, these significant cost advantage will help the company to capture high market share. Sometimes we called this a natural monopoly.

Cost of Expansion

When a company is expanding very fast, its cost of production may be significantly increased. If the revenue of the firm can't grow as fast as the cost. The company's profit level may drop.

Cost of finance

Some firms may be capital intensive such as property developers. They may borrow billion of loans to finance their property development projects. Some huge property developers can borrow more than 100billion for their new investments. The change in the cost of borrowing like a higher interest rate will significantly affect the company's financial performance. They will become highly interest-sensitive, a one percent change in the borrowing interest may significantly affect the company's financial performance. They can take advantage of lower rates when the market interest rate drops.

Tax Changes

Changes in corporate tax and other business-related taxes can heavily affect the company's profitability. If the corporate tax cut is 10%, it means the company can save 10% of their total profit, this can significantly improve their profitability indicator. Therefore, now you know why the US market has been significantly raised in 2017. The market Is mainly benefited by the US government 's tax reform which increased those firms' profitability.

Profit Growth Analysis

A company can increase its profit level by increasing sales or reducing the cost of production. We should understand that cost reduction has its limits. Therefore, profit growth mainly caused by sales growth generally can enjoy a higher valuation level than a company generates the same amount of profit by cost-cutting only.

The gross profit means the sales revenue minus the direct cost of production. Some mobile phone manufacturer has a very low gross profit (<10%), after deduction of the indirect cost the firm mostly like won't have much profit or even suffer loss. After deducting all the tax and related fees, the net profit is the amount that the firm can distribute to its shareholders as a dividend or keep it as retained profit for future usage.

Some firms need to pay for a high proportion of cost on some input with high price uncertainty such as oil prices. Therefore, the profit of the airline industry will become unpredictable in advance.

In contrast, if you are analyzing a water supply company(or power plants of renewable resources) in a region, the demand and the cost of steady, this kind of company can generate stable profit if the local government does not have strict price control.

But the limitation is such kind of firm maybe lack growth potential unless they invest in some other firms in a similar industry. These kinds of merges sometimes may not be a good deal if they need to pay for a high premium to purchase new assets.

Sometimes profit is not generated from operating business, but such profits can significantly affect the company's financial statement. If a company hold a lot of investment asset such as properties of shares for trading, the asset valuation change may significantly affect the company's profit level without any cash related benefit involved.

For example, a company holds a shopping mall in a region, the shopping mall 's estimated value of the current year increased by 10 million. If the company does not intend to sell it to the market, or the market do not have such a buyer who is willing to buy it at such price level. That kind of profit is just some accounting profit in the accounting book, and it is not hard to use or distribute as you don't have any cash flow involved.

If the company is a multi-national company with a high proportion of sales in a foreign country, the foreign currency exchange Gain (/Loss) item may be a significant factor affecting the profit level in the income statement. In contrast, a company may record currency exchange loss when their foreign currency-denominated income faced a significant depreciation in the current year, and these most likely happen in some emerging countries.

Understand the ROE

ROE is a very important profitability indicator in our financial world. ROA will join used together with the ROA to assess the financial performance of a company.

A company with a higher ROE means that the company can earn how high return level with its own equity. For the manufacturing firms, their ROE normally will be lower than 10. The financial industry like banks previously ROE can be higher than 15, but now most of them are lower than 10. The European banks suffer from negative yields which their performance is even worse. However, for some tech-related firms like Apple or Microsoft, their ROE can be higher than 30. It means that those tech-related firms are more profitable than other industry, they can earn a higher return with the same amount of shareholder's capital.

Understanding ROA

A company can increase its ROE by increasing borrowing, but too much borrowing may not be a good idea as the business risk will be increasing. Therefore, we will also check for the Return of assets (ROA) for the company as a reference.

ROA x leverage = ROE

If a company can earn a high ROE but with a very low ROA ratio, it means the company borrowing a lot. If the industry is booming, too much borrowing may not be a problem. But once the industry is declining or the cost of borrowing is significantly raised. That kind of company will easily underperform the market.

Understanding EPS growth

Earnings per share growth is another important consideration for an investor. A company without any sales and profit growth can keep on increasing its EPS by stock repurchase. The amount of stock repurchase is higher than one trillion USD in 2019. The company itself is the biggest buyer in the stock market.

The long-term stock price trend will be affected by its EPS growth, the higher the growth rate, the higher the potential benefit of investing in such stock. This is a must know indicator for an investor.

Understanding the dividend yield rate

The dividend is the cash benefit distributed to the shareholder when the firm can earn some profit. The dividend level for most of the firms in the US market tends to be quite low (at 1-2%). This is because the dividend is subject to the income tax.

For some region without dividend related income tax, the dividend payout ratio can be higher, the yield can be higher than 4% in general. A firm with a higher dividend payout ratio doesn't mean it can be performed better, it just means the firm does not need to keep too much cash as working capital or for new investments. For a growth stock, the dividend ratio tends to be lower than 1% or zero, Amazon seldom paid a dividend to the shareholder, but shareholders will not mind due to the persistent raising of the share price.

Balance Sheet Analysis

We should understand the basic idea of the balance sheet

Asset - Liability = Shareholder 's equity

We can understand that the company's book value is based on its net asset.

For example, if you opened a transport company that only has five trucks as assets. You used your company's name to borrow 100% the value of the trucks from your friends. Your asset (trucks) will be equals to your liability (borrowing from friends), your company does not have any shareholder's equity. The book value of your firm is zero when it startup. This example shows a company with lots of assets doesn't mean it has high accounting equities, it depends on its liability level, also the profitability.

If your company can earn a profit based on your good

management, the profit remained in the company is considered as shareholder's equity. A company with more assets doesn't mean it will have higher profitability. It may just mean the company has lots of liability need to be repaid and a higher cost of finance.

For an individual investor, it is too time-consuming to understand different balance sheet items. We can focus on some key items only to save time.

Debts Level Analysis
The higher the debts level, the higher the cost of finance.
If the operational cash flow is not sufficient to pay for the debts. The company needs to raise more new loans or issue more equity to finance for the cost.

An investor can also review the company's short-term liability level with the current assets including cash. If the current asset including cash in hand is too low, the company may have liquidity problems if they are not able to obtain short-term finance. If a company can't have enough cash flow to repay their short-term debts in the coming year, the firm will have high liquidity risk. The worst case is bankruptcy.

If a company have enough short-term cash flow but accumulating many long-term debts, you better notice what years most of the debts will be mature which need to repay the debts. The firm will be at higher risk in such years if they can't obtain new loans or new sources of finance.

Cash Flow Analysis

For Cash flow, an investor does not need to consider too much. You only need to have a look at the cash flow from the operational activity, checking whether is it reasonably matching with the revenue and profit. If the value in the cash flow statement is significantly lower than the income statement, it means that the profit may come from some no-cash items such as the revaluation of assets, or accumulated a lot of accounts receivable which may need to be written off in the future.

Cash flow from investing activity normally will be a negative value due to the company needs to spend more on new investment.
If the company's operating cash flow always be negative, it may not be a good phenomenon. It only needs the cash flow from financing activity to support. You will find that the cash flow from financing activity always is positive. You should notice that the firms may not be able to be self-sufficient by its cash. They have a

demand for refinancing in the future.

Stock Momentum

About the Momentum Factor

If a stock market 's price mainly driven by some noise factor (Momentum Factor), value investment or any fundamental investor is very difficult to outperformance the market.

If no one is trading based on fundamental factors, the factors become irrelevant for the market 's short to medium-term performance. It will only affect the long-term bottom line of the market. If the fundamental factors are improving, the bottom of the stock market will keep on rising in the long run.

Therefore, trading in such kind of market should focus more on the Momentum Factor, which is the main driving factor in the market instead of the fundamental changes. The rule is very important, especially when you are trading in such a typical "go-go" and "die-hard" market. The investor with an emerging market trading experience will understand what I am talking about.

If some market seems not easy to take profit in the long run, why don't we ignore it? If you remember what I stated before when too much money will be tracing for too little real asset, the market will be driven by the noise factors. In history, the emerging market will suddenly have a market boom after the developed market started their engines. This is because when the developed market moved to a plateau without further growing momentum, many investors will move their eyes to the emerging markets.

If the age of negative yields happened to the US market, the emerging market might eventually take benefit from it if the emerging market still can provide a certain level of positive yield. The bond market will take the advantage first, you will find that the yields of the emerging market sovereignty bond be significantly lowered. This is a good signal for the market is favor for risky assets and seeking less risk premium. Then the emerging stock market will eventually be improved as well. Now you may know why I use so many chapters to explain the character of different markets.

Trade Volume (Liquidity)

Liquidity level of a stock is a very important concern for any investors. If you would like to invest a stock that lack of liquidity, the first problem will be the bid-ask spread. You can lose money easily by buying and selling the share during a short trading period.

The liquidity level is also an important concern for the ETF trader.

If your ETF has poor liquidity, you will find that very hard to find enough buyers or sellers if you want to trade in bulk. You may need to purchase it at a premium price far higher than its Net Asset Value or sell it below its NAV.

If you find the market price is quite good, but you are not able to find buyers or need to sell it at a bargain price. The market price movement is quite meaningless for you. Therefore, most of the institutional investor will not consider stocks with poor liquidity.

Price Trend

The most important thing in momentum analysis is the price trend, is the major market price trend mainly moving up or down?

Uptrend

This is very simple to understand for the price trend. In the below diagram, each time when the market has adjustments, the bottom level of the adjustment is increasing to a higher level. This refers to an uptrend pattern.

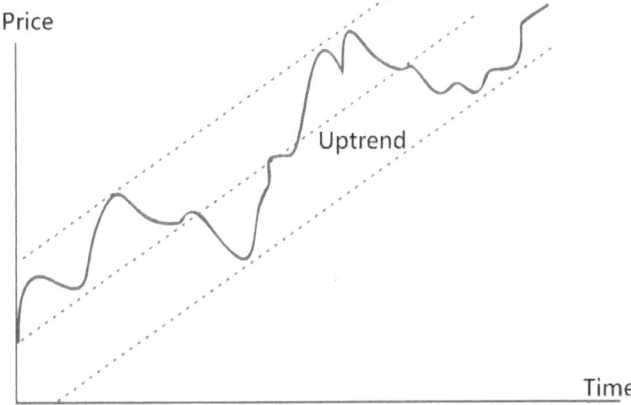

Downtrend

The concept of downtrend is very similar to an uptrend. In the below diagram, each time when the market has rebounded, the highest level of the adjustment is decreasing to a lower level. This refers to a downtrend pattern.

Price Reference point: Support / Resistant

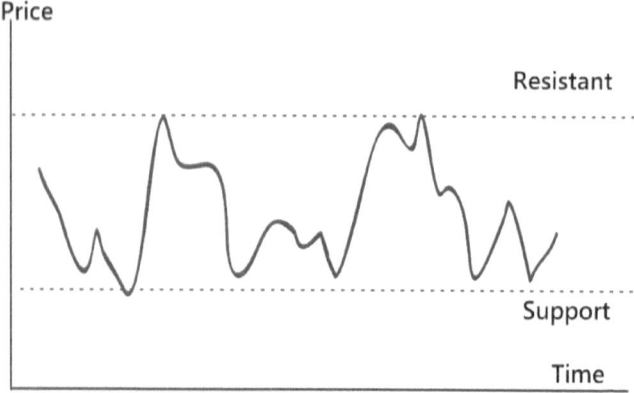

Resistant refers to the market can't break through a certain price level. Many sellers would like to sell their stocks when the price is close to the resistant level, the selling pressure will be increased when the price is closer to the resistant level.

Support refers to the market stopped declining at a certain price level. If the market tried several times still can't break the supporting level, many investors might consider the market may reach the short-term bottom.

Breakthrough

If the stock price can break the resistant after serval times of trial, and it further raised to a new level, we will call this kind of trading pattern as a breakthrough. However, some breakthrough cases may eventually become a failure attempt, and the stock doesn't have any further momentum to go up and drop back below the previous resistant level. If the price keeps going down, it will trigger many investors' cut loss actions.

The return for some successful breakthrough may be big, but the accuracy of such a pattern is not good enough.

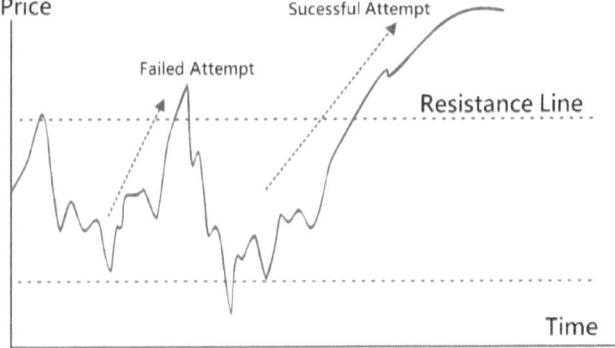

Moving Average

Moving Average is a popular indicator of trading. If a stock is in increasing trend which is higher than its 200 days average, it indicates the stock is moving in a long-term uptrend. Some traders may consider cutting loss when the stock price is lower than 200 days average.

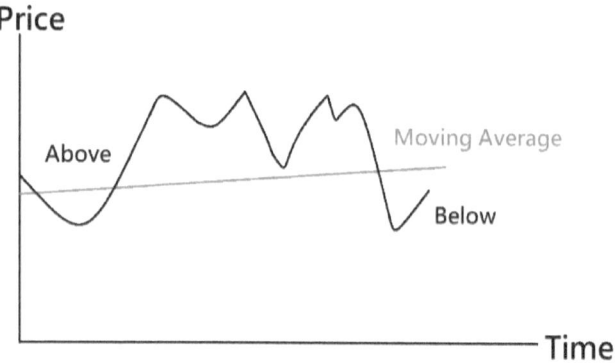

For the medium-term traders, they may consider a 50-day average or 20-day average. If you are traders in emerging markets or any markets that have high fluctuation levels, traders tend to use shorter days (10 or 20 days) moving average as trading reference. This is because when the stock price is moving quickly, the investor who uses some long-term moving average as an indicator will have serious lagging effects. Therefore, shorter days moving average will have higher reference value in such a market.

RSI

RSI is a very popular technical indicator. If the RSI 's value is greater than 70, it means the stock is overbought. The stock will have a higher chance to have short-term adjustment shortly.

If the RSI value is below 30, it means the stock is oversold. The stock will have a higher chance to have short-term rebound in the future.

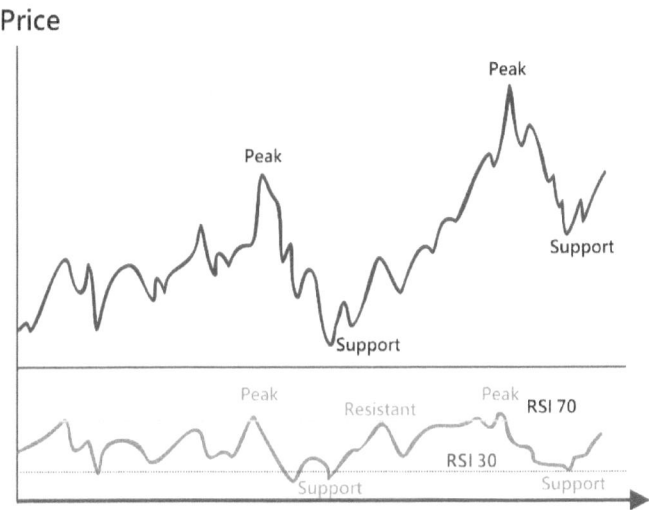

When we are checking the stock diagram with the RSI indicator, you can easily find that each time the stock price increased from the bottom, the RSI will start from a relatively low level. In contrast, when the stock price is closer to the peak, the RSI will be at a relatively higher level. You will feel that the RSI have certain prediction ability.

In reality, the RSI is not able to predict the long-term price trend.

If the stock price keeps on decreasing, the RSI can decrease from 35 to 30, then 30 to 25, then 25 to 20. You can never know in advance whether RSI reached 30 is the bottom or not. It only can tell you that the selling pressure of the stock is quite high.

If we use the RSI in trading for some countries' ETF, you will notice that some market using RSI below 30 as an entry reference can be profitable. For example, if you apply the RSI index the Hong Kong 's Hang Seng index (a typical emerging market) 's weekly diagram, you can find it is profitable each time when the RSI is very close or below 30. Buy stocks at the RSI below 30 may be able to make a profit for some market which has cycling fluctuation features.

The stock market 's base value remained at a certain trading range, but it's price level have a certain degree of cyclical fluctuations during a 3 to 5-year trading cycle. An investor can take advantage when they buy in a lower range and sell it later. But sometime the market will move to a deep bottom before it climbs back. Such kind of opportunity is not suitable for all investors.

For some market like the US which the market index rarely will have big drops, it's not suitable to apply such kind of practice.

MACD

MACD is a popular technical indicator for stock investing. It is tracking the price movement momentum of the stock. If the EMA fast line cut through and stay above the EMA slow line, it means the stock is moving at an increasing stage. However, if the fast EMA cut the slow EMA at a very high price level, it may refer that the stock price may be lacking further growth momentum. Some investor may consider quitting their position to take profit, and this can lead to some technical selling pressure.

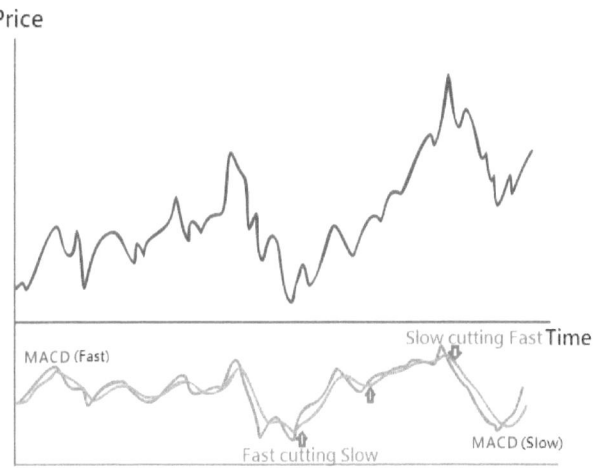

MACD can be an excellent indicator if the stock is just starting a major price trend, but it will become useless when the stock price has a certain level of random fluctuations without any major price trend. The main problem is, we can never know whether this time is a major price change or just a small degree of changes in advance.

MACD is suitable to use for some big events which may lead to a medium to long-term growth uptrend in the future. It is also suitable for some market that is dominated by noise traders, which most of the market player completely ignored the fundamental factors. The MACD will become an important indicator for investor 's reference in such market, as many market trader will take actions based on some technical indicator changes, they want to be the first one to escape from a big zero-sum game which can take most of the profit home. Therefore, the momentum factor will become very important (or even decisive factor) in such a market.

Limitations of Momentum factor analysis
Using momentum factor or technical factor for trading reference is very easy, everyone can buy some technical analysis book and starting their analysis within a few hours' "training".

However, using such a reference to earning income persistently is very difficult. The main problem is all the technical indicator 's accuracy is not high, mainly below 50%.

In some period when the market has some big price movement, you will find that the momentum factor becomes very useful. However, in some other period, use the momentum factor to trade will become playing with a money burner, as trading with momentum factors will already lead to a cut loss action. History will repeat itself, but history will not always be the same.

Therefore, past patterns or experience may not be suitable for the future. Whenever you use any criteria for stock trading, remember that they may not always lead to good results, you need to prepare for the worst.

If we can take profit from the momentum factor, why not?
However,
- The result is too random
- Past cannot predict the future
- history may not repeat itself

Therefore, the momentum factor can be a reference factor, but better not be a decisive factor

Capture the Alpha

The Art of Security Analysis

Studying thousands of stocks in the market is very time consuming, and the value-added for such kind of security analysis may be very little. So why do we need to spend our valuable time to do something that may be meaningless unless for killing out leisure time? However, if some simple ideas can improve our investing performance in the long run without using too much time for analysis. Why not have a look at it? This kind of action is called seeking the Alpha in the market.

Think about a deep question, if the stock market purely reflects the fundamental business factors why many stocks have more than 2% intraday movement without any new factors changes?

The answer is simple. Many other factors will affect the stock price movement. If you consider the fundamental business factor condition as the core factor, the other factors as noise. The change in core factor only can explain for 10-30% of movements in different academic studies. This finding is very interesting; what the market believes as value investment or fundamental analysis does not add too much value for predicting short to medium term changes of the stock price.

Let us look back at the 1987 stock crash, the major stock index dropped more than 20% in one trading day without any significant fundamental factors is changed. The initial price drops triggered selling pressure and led to a further price drop, and the Stock futures market was also adding some extra selling pressures in the market. Peter Lynch, one of the most famous fund managers in the 1980s' who managed a multi-billion investment giant Magellan Fund mentioned in his writing that he couldn't predict such stock crash in advance. If he still can't, do you think that you can predict it in advance?

Many readers may say that they know the stock price was overpriced in 1987. The market index raised almost 30% earlier in 1987. But the main point is, it seems over-priced when the market raised by 5%, 10%, 20%, 30%... So, you will quit the market when it raised 5%, and sitting there waiting for the market adjustment, 5%, 10%,25%... You only know the stock market raised 30% earlier that year, a price adjustment may be coming soon, but you never know when and how strong it is in advance.

If you are smart enough (or lucky enough) that sell all your stocks at the highest level before the crash, do you still have the courage to buy stocks immediately after the crash, the market has golden decade after the 1987 stock crash, the return is more than a double in the future.

If we look at all the studies, the correlation between fundamental factors and the stock market performance may become stronger in the long run in some developed market. Such markets have a good eco-system that good company's value will eventually reflect in the stock price. Many of the most innovative firms with high profitability are listed in the US stock market in the past. That's why stock for the long run works in the US market for the past years. If a market does not have innovative and profitable firms joined, it 's long-term return potential will be relatively lower, the opportunity of investing such a market only happens when the stock market becomes a bargain, or some structural reform is introduced by the government which can improve the long-term profitability of the listed companies.

Traditional valuation tools for a stock

Understanding the P/E Ratio

The Price-earnings ratio is a typical indicator we used to assess the valuation level of the stock.

Price to Earnings Ratio (P/E):

$$\frac{\text{Stock Price}}{\text{Earnings per share}}$$

In theory, the higher the P/E ratio means the firms are more expensive than other firms with lower P/E.

P/E is a good indicator for comparing the relative value during the different market cycle. The US market 's average P/E is around 12-14 times in the last century, but now is at around 20 times, it means that the valuation of the US market is towards its upper limit now. This does not indicate that the stock market will sudden drop or the market must back to its normal range very soon. It indicates the long-term profit potential when you enter the market right now. If the market is trading at 30 times which is higher than before, are they driven by earning growth? Do monetary environment changes drive them? How much room the market can growth if I invest it right now?

P/E can use as an inter-market comparison. You will find that the emerging market general trade at a lower P/E than the developed market as investors will need some risk premium to compensate for their risk. However, when the emerging market is in a boom cycle, the valuation and P/E can be significantly higher than the developed market, the P/E can be as high as 50 -100 times. It is crazy in terms of valuation. Then you know that it will not be a good time to enter the market.

In the traditional viewpoint, the lower the P/E values mean that stock price is more attractive; the logic is simple. A stock 's P/E value is five means that the company's stock price is trading as five times its accounting price per share during the current financial year. The average P/E of the US stock market (S&P) is around 12 to 16. The P/E can become 16 to 20 in a bull market, and it can be even higher than 25 in some extreme market phase.

During a recession, the companies' profit level may be significantly deteriorated. Like the case of 2008, as many of the first suffer loose, the market P/E can be higher than 40 in a certain period. Therefore, the P/E ratio will become useless during a recession as many of the firms may even record losses in that period. We will better use the P/B indicator as reference.

Using P/E for reference is an art, it never means that a stock with 20 times P/E will underperform the stock with 10 times P/E in the same industry. We need to use a competitive viewpoint based on the growth potential.

You should notice that if the monetary policy is quite loose in a period, or the profit growth rate is faster, the P/E ratio will be higher at around 20 or above level in a long period. For example, the case of the 1990s, the stock index kept on climbing up, the lowest valuation appeared in 1994 at around 16 P/E after an adjustment, then it climbed above the 20 until the burst of the dot-com bubble in the year 2000.

Price to Book Ratio (P/B)

$$\frac{\text{Stock Price}}{\text{Book Value per Share}}$$

The book value means the accounting value of the firms. If the company's price is traded more than four times its book value. You may consider the market is giving a very good price to the s. P/B is a very good indicator when trading in the bear market. Generally, the bottom of a stock crash is P/B around 1. But it may only happen once in 20 years, or even never happen. For the US market, the general P/B Range is 2.5 to 3.5. For tech-related firms, the P/B will be far higher to around 5 to 10 as the teach firms generally do not have too much-fixed assets. P/B around 1.5 to 2 already be quite speculative for the US market. For some leading emerging countries, PB value will have chances to trade at around 1 per 10 years horizon. That is a good entry time for long-term investment.

Sales and Profit Growth

A company with a higher sales growth rate in the past years will be considered having higher growth potential in the future. Their valuations will be generally higher. The company may not need to have profit growth together, and a persistent sales growth already can attract many market funding even the company cannot earn any profit till now. Investors will think about the example of Amazon, the price of shares mare likely reflecting its sales ability, whether than its profitability. We will discuss the details of Cost and Revenue analysis in the individual firm analysis chapter.

Experienced Investors will not make their investment decision solely by their valuation level. A company with low P/E and P/B doesn't mean it is a better investment option than a company with high P/E and P/B. If a company's main business is shrinking, the stock will have high selling pressure. If the falling in stock price is faster than the profit, then it will look like a "value" investment.

But they are cheap because they should be cheap!

Competitive value viewpoint

Buy the share with higher **competitive value is a good idea.** This is the way that Warrant Buffet has beaten the market in before. Many people know that Benjamin is the teacher of Warrant Buffet, but you should know that Philip A. Fisher highly influences Warrant Buffet later with the concepts of buying growth stocks at a good price. The concept of competitive value means that buying the stock with better growth potential in the long run at a reasonable price.

E.g. for stock with similar P/E and P/B level in the same industry, the stock with better ROE, higher sales and profit growth prediction is more attractive

If you compare a stock to the market average, some stocks may beat the market in the long run due to its long-term growth nature. But the average buying price is the most important factor that affects your profitability for a profitable item. Think about what happens if you buy shares in the dot-com bubble in the year 2000, you may lose 95% of your investment in the worst period.

The tech-related stock index needed more than ten years to recover the loss.

But I must remind my readers that it is not easy to find a cheap growth stock in a bull market. We are not in the 1970s or 1980s, and we are now at an age that lots of financial institutions with computer AI to analyze thousands of stocks with quantitative methods. The bargain price only appears during "market sales (Bear market)"; if you find a bargain growth share in a bull market, you may be most likely buy garbage or buy shares that are lacking liquidity because they are cheap in any market conditions.

Don't rely on any stock pricing Model

Some investors who loved the fundamental analysis always image they are the next Warren Buffet by stock selection. This is a age that the stock market crowded of hedge funds, and institutional investors. Many of them have different kinds of quantitative experts for stock selection. Their trading machine are aimed for any minor mispricing opportunities, except for those stock without liquidity (stock which is lacking buyer and sellers).

Do you think that you still can easily find opportunities by simply reading some financial report by yourself? Even Warren Buffet also holds more than a hundred billion of idled cash. He can't find enough investment opportunity too. Earning the market return is far easier and more practical for most of the investor. If you still want to manage your portfolio actively, stock portfolio selections (like ETFs with a different theme) and market timing is the easiest way to capture the Alpha return. Fundamental analysis for individual stocks selection is not easy to generate extra profit.

As an investment book, I will still introduce you that basic valuation methods for reference. Let you know that those "professional figures" actually come from what kind of basic ideas. In our traditional investment textbook, we can calculate the "fair value" of a stock based on the below models

The discount cash flow model (Optional)

The present value of an asset

$$= \frac{CF0 + CF1}{1+k} + \frac{CF2}{(1+k)^2} + \frac{CS3}{(1+k)^3} \cdots$$

CF0 = The immediate cash flow after purchase normally is zero
CF1 = cash flow of the next payment date
CF2 = Cash Flow of the second payment date
K = Necessary return of an asset

Adding up all the projected income together and discount its future value into present income. Don't worry that if you don't understand the formula, it is for reference only. The actual idea is quite simple if at the end of this year can receive $10.5 dividend per share if we assume the K return is 5%. The present value of the dividend will be $10 ($10.5/105%). If at the end of next year can earn 11, discounted as present value is $ 9.98, the calculation will go on to the third year.

If you finally find the fair price of the stock should be $150 after you have discounted all the future dividend into present value. The current price of the stock is $120. The stock price seems to undervalue, and you may purchase it as you believe it is undervalued.

However, after you purchased the stock, its price keeps going down, now becomes $100 only. You may think that the market is further miss pricing, then, you buy more. However, it further drops to $90. What 's wrong with your investment model?

You model is not wrong, but only you trust for it. Who cares about your "fair price" except for yourself In the real stock market? If you are not able to influence the stock price, you need to be waiting for someone to pull up the price level. If none of them will trade the stock based on your calculation, you will find that your stock model fooled yourself. Model is a model, and the market is a market — the model used in the academic field for us to understand how something works. However, the model doesn't work in the stock market unless most of the traders know and believed in the models' projected value.

In some occasions, the model value calculated form some financial institution's analyst worked well during an extreme bull market. This is because many newcomers who are just joined the stock market totally believed in the analyst 's model prediction, they will use such a figure as their trading reference. Then the model value really can affect the market price. But obviously, it is not related to your calculation. Give up some useless attempt to calculate the market, use the time to understand how it works is more meaningful.

Dividend Growth Model (Optional)

$$= \frac{D1}{r-g}$$

D1 = Expected dividend return at the end of the year

r = The necessary return of stock investment

g = Dividend growth rate

Another typical valuation model is the dividend growth model. The pricing model added the growth factors into the model, makes it more meaningful. However, how can you know the growth rate of next year, the third year...

Even you are the boss of the company you will not know what the business environment will be changed in the next year unless you are operating power plants or water supply business. The growth rate for business is uncertain, the discount rate (depends on the market interest) is uncertain, the market response is uncertain; the only certainty thing is everything are uncertain!

PEG Model (Optional)

$$\frac{P/E \text{ Ratio}}{\text{EPS Growth Rate}}$$

PEG calculation is another popular analysis of the growth potential of a company. The lower the value of the PEG means the stock price is more attractive in terms of growth. In the model, a stock with a 0.8 PEG value is less attractive with another stock with 0.5 PEG value. But the main problem is, the growth rate of a firm is always changing. Therefore, the PEG value can use as a reference only. It should not consider as a serious indicator.

All the above model values can be used as a reference only. You should not use as a decisional consideration. Never 100% trust any models, historical performance or price patterns. I agree that the market always repeated itself. But the market sometimes surprises all the players and make a new, unexpected pattern, and each time may be different. The old record will be break by the new one! Don't be kicked out from the market by an unexpected event or your misunderstanding about the market.

Core factor and Noise factor - Individual Stock Analysis

Besides the stock model or indicators, we can use some additional tools for stock analysis. We will analyze the factors that drive price changes with core and noise factors. Noise factor sometimes is a dominating factor for the price movement in some market.

1) Core Fundamental Factors

Fundamental changes are predictable and transparent for investors

You can use models to explain most of the long-term price trend e.g. Growth stocks focus on sales per shares growth

e.g. Value stocks focus on steady profit growth and dividend yield level, the stock repurchase scheme

Fundamental factors are more likely to be the dominating factors for the long-term stock price movements for those market stars with high liquidity levels.

2) Noise Factors (/Market Trading Factors)
Predictable price movement pattern (Momentum factors)
Unpredictable factors.
Noise factors are more likely to dominate the stock price changes for those Small to medium-sized stocks which are lack of liquidity.

We need to learn some valuation tools before we think about how to capture the Alpha

Learn how to capture the Alpha

There is some simple strategy that could help to capture the Alpha. The main assumption is the stock market will be growing in the long run, and the market index will mainly reflect for fundamental factors changes

Market / Stock Selection

Select Stocks with high long-term competitive value by assess its profitability potential. The fundamental factors show how good companies are performing. However, for investors, another more important concern is the price.

A good investment is:

Good company with good pricing

A bad investment is:

Good company in bad pricing

Bad company in bad pricing

A Fair investment is:

Good company with fair pricing

Speculative investment is:

Bad company in good pricing

Gamble for Black Swan Event – Betting for some low possibility event such as Brexit, you have a fair chance to win big when Black Swan appears.

Market Timing

The lower the price of the price index, the higher the long-run average return.

(Market Timing Alpha)

- Buy more when the stock market is around the bottom
- Reduce your net position or at least stop adding new investments when the market is overheated.

Capture for the Momentum

Using fundamental analysis as a basic selection, use price trends (Uptrend or a major price breakthrough) as confirmation, follow the price movement of the market. Especially capture the medium trend growth due to some fundamental factors changes.

Events Bonus – Some events that will have some long-term fundamental changes that will benefit from the long run. E.g. If a trade conflict is eased, new investment plants can go-ahead as business confidence will be improved.

Reform Bonus - A new government that will make market reforms and promotes long-term investment is elected. This will lead to long-term economic growth in the economy with some potential investment opportunities.

Monetary Bonus – The Central bank decided to adopt a more aggressive monetary policy, lowering the interest rate and increase the money supply in the long run. This is a long-term investment green light for investors. Some central banks like the Bank of Japan may even directly purchase ETF in the stock market. If the central bank would like to send some money into your pocket, why not open your bag and receive it!

Size of the portfolio and investment performance

If your portfolio size is big enough, you are not easy to earn an extra return. You can only select those big company shares with excellent liquidity if you invest in small firms, the proportion of investment will be very little, even the return is very high, but the overall contribution to your whole portfolio will be insignificant. (e.g. 1 million return for a 10 Billion portfolio). Therefore, your portfolio's investment return will be similar to the market return (Beta).

Many people know that Warren Buffet is one of the most famous investors in the last 50 years. Seldom have people think about why so little people can copy his strategy and become as successful as him. The main point is, the good time is gone. It means that you are not able to travel back to the 1980s or 1990s to earn huge excess returns from the market.

Warren Buffet 's investment return after the 2008 Global Financial crisis is quite similar to the S&P 500 index. That means you can only earn the market return by copying his same portfolio. It also means that you are not able to attract investors to set up new funds by giving them such kind of market return. Another point is that you don't own an insurance company that has lots of "floats" insurance funds that can use for long-term investing with very low cost of finance.

When your size of the investment is big enough, you will become the market itself. You cannot earn returns higher than the market itself as you are the same body. That's one of the important principles from *Winning the losers' game* written by Charles D. Ellis. If you have time, have a look for this book, also recommend for reading the *Random Walk down the wall street* written by Burton G. Malkiel, both books are valuable for your time and money. The core idea of the two books are very simple, when the investment funds and institutional investor become bigger and bigger, they are now the dominating players in the market and almost become the market itself. It is not possible to generate an excess return from such kind of market.

I agree with some of the viewpoints in those books. But don't forget that one way to capture the Alpha is from the market mispricing, especially during a bear market with lots of forced selling. If you can provide liquidity for good investment items during crisis time, you can obtain the Alpha from the market. Howard Marks built up a speculative bond portfolio with extremely bargain pricing during the global financial crisis in 2008-2009.

Another way to capture market Alpha is by earning money from other investors. There are many active market players such as hedge funds. Their profit and loss not based on the market index changes. They are always setting different market positions, sometimes is very similar to gambling. They will gamble anything that can earn a positive expected return in their quantitative model based on statistics.

As they believe in statistics, we can take advantage of such kind of statistics as well. The market always underestimates the risk when the market price is going up. The VIX index, which shows the expected volatility (market risk) is at an extremely low level (below 10) during early 2018. You can buy cheap options as protection for your portfolio. The 1% insurance cost can save you more than 10% downside risk. We will discuss how to use options as protection at the end of this little book. You can keep your stock for the long run portfolio with very low risk if the volatility market offers you a good price for stock portfolio protections. You may say thank you to such kind of statistical trader who offers you opportunities to earn an excess return (Alpha) from the market.

Rational ignorance – Only aim for the market return

If you enjoy the market return and don't want to take the risk and use up your own leisure time to actively manage your portfolio, you can purchase the major stock index fund to capture the Beta.

Remind that you should use a diversified portfolio to earn the market return. If your own countries' stock market is very small and lack of growing momentum, why not consider investing in the developed market 's major stock market index such as MSCI World. This kind of index will capture the most representative companies in the portfolio.

If you don't imagine you can beat the market, major stock index ETF is a kind of good investment option. Individual stock analysis is a very difficult and time-consuming activity. Rational ignorance sometimes is a reasonable choice, especially in a developed market that larger stocks outperform smaller sized stocks. Save time, enjoy the market return is a good choice for many investors.

The Bango Stocks

The Story of Bango Stocks

Warning! All the below cases are stories with a survival basis. We use these two cases to discuss what are the features of the Bango stocks. Don't believe that what you invest can generate a similar return in the future.

The case of Apple (AAPL)

Apple is a typical example of Bongo stocks. You can earn more than 20000% of return when you invested in 2003. Even you are very unlucky that purchase at the peak of the tech-stock bubble in 2000, you still can earn a 5000% return till now.

Do you still remember what apple is making 20 years before, the Mac computer with a big screen? They started to make a music player called the iPod, and the iPod is unexpectedly successful. Then they make a phone with the iPod 's user interface, the iPhone in 2007. This phone completely changed the industry. Don't tell me that you can expect Apple will become the world 's most profitable mobile phone producer in the year 2000.

Apple is a typical example of a company that changed its business models. Changing the business model is the biggest factor to support the long-term growth in the stock market. Although changing business model may lead to failure as well, it is like a coin will have two sides. It may make an old company become a new market star, or it may make a poor company losing its capital at a faster rate.

Therefore, if a stock index does not have some new and energetic firms are joining in, existing firms will not change their business model to capture any new growth potential, the stock market index will not grow even the economy is growing. This is the fundamental reason why stock for the long run doesn't work in many emerging markets.

The case of Tencent
Tencent is a legend for stock investment, the company listed in the Hong Kong stock exchange for around HKD $3 in 2003, and now it trades at an actual value at more than $1500 (1 stock split to 5 previously). The return is more than 50000% with the dividend reinvestment for a long-term investor. What you need to do is buy and hold. But the main point is how can you know the share price can climb to such level when you invested in the company in 2003.

The company even can't find a good business model that can generate good profit in that year. They are struggling for survival issue.

They eventually find some new ways to turn the users into profit, created many leading apps that have billions of users. Therefore, this stock becomes a legend, no because it is great at IPO, it is because they become great after IPO. The shareholders can enjoy the benefits of business growth and valuation improvement. If the company already be great when it is launching an IPO, the IPO price will be "fair" enough for both parties. It means you can't expect strong growth potential in a short period. This investment may become "tasteless" for an investor.

Now you know that the best return always comes from unexpected changing the business model. The ultra-high return stocks always have some unpredictable business model changes or new positive business factors changes that drive the completely changed the long-term growth potential.

If you purchase a new IPO stock, the valuation of the firm is 200 billion, how far it can grow? The market and industry have its maximum limits. The returns will be very little if the market already "Price-in" its maximum growth limit. Overpriced IPO is one of the reasons why many emerging market 's stock index can't grow in the long run. There isn't too much room for investors to earn after it list in the stock exchange, the stock may be overdraft certain years' growth potential.

In 2018, early the Tencent 's stock price was peaked at around 470, but it dropped to around 250 in late October in the same year. A Bango stock doesn't mean that it will always be climbing up, such kind of stocks may also have high volatility. Buying Bango stock at peak or when it is fully price-in the future growth may not be a good long term investment option.

Some speculative shares can rise very fast without profit or even sales growth to support, please avoid such kind of zero-sum game. If you are a risk lover, you can use a small proportion of funding to join the game with preparation for a total loss. Never use 100% capital in a single speculative investment object.

No matter how many times you become the winner in the games, you will lose everything with one fatal investment!

Some Important Ideas

Understand the compound interest effects

Compound interest effect is one of the miracle effects that can generate for long-term returns. Let's look at the below examples.

4% Dividend available for reinvestment

Year	1	2	3	4	5	6	7	8
Pricniple	100	100	100	100	100	100	100	100
Dividend	4	4	4	4	4	4	4	4
End of year principle with dividend reinvesting	104	108.2	112.5	117	121.7	126.5	131.6	136.8

Assume that you invested in a stock that can provide 4% of dividend return each year.

After eight years of principle reinvestment, your principle becomes 136.8, and each year your dividend amount increased to $5.2 instead of $4 at the begin. And what you need to do is just sitting there and do nothing, it is like waiting for your fruit plant growing.

7% Dividend available for reinvestment

Year	1	2	3	4	5	6	7	8
Pricniple -Beginning	100	100	100	100	100	100	100	100
Dividend	7	7	7	7	7	7	7	7
End of year principle with dividend reinvesting	107	114.5	122.5	131.1	140.3	150.1	160.6	171.8

Assume that you invested in a stock that can provide 7% of dividend return each year.

After eight years of principle reinvestment, your principle becomes 171.8, and each year your dividend amount increased to $11.2 instead of $7 at the begin. The above shows the miracle of compound interest.

Companies that pay out high dividend yields generally will have a slower growth rate. This is because the company will have less capital available for future investment after distributing the cash dividends. If the profit of the company is steady, continuously reinvesting the dividend for more shares will keep on increasing your yield return.

Investors can use such reinvestment tactics to enjoy compound interest effect, that kind of trading strategy is very popular in some Asian Stocks market which the stocks already lack growing momentums. Individual Investor will choose some company that can generate a steady profit as their targets (like utilities or some state-owned banks), they can enjoy around 4 to 5% return per annualized return with such kind of reinvestment strategy.

However, once the company faces any significant change in the business environment or sudden change in law or regulations. The investor may suffer huge due to the portfolio is too concentrated. The case of the UK Northern Rock Bank is typical, some of the employees even put most of their pensions to buy the bank's shares. When the bank eventually collapsed after the global financial crisis in 2008, the long-term investor and those employees suffered hugely. That's why I never recommend investors to put their pension in a highly concentrated portfolio. It may be too dangerous, as you will not have time to earn money back after you suffer huge unforeseeable loss in a few concentrated investments.

Beware of Financial Fakery

As an individual investor, we are not able to identify all the financial fakery. But financial fakery is quite easy to observe, their financial performance is too unreasonable.

For investors who choose portfolio investment like invest in some major market index, financial fakery is not a big concern as the failure of one or a few firms may not have too harmful effects on your portfolio. Therefore, I quite recommend investors who do not have time to manage their investment used some index-based investment instead of trading individual shares by themselves. Alternatively, you can trade a few shares you are quite familiar outside your stock index portfolio. The main reasons are financial fakery or some unexpected event that can significantly harm your portfolio's return.

Even the institutional investor can't avoid some financial fakery or being harm from some unexpected events. That's why diversify a portfolio is a good idea for most of the investor. I understand the highest return comes from some Bango shares which we will discuss in the previous chapter in this book, if you concentrated on holding such shares, you could beat all the market players. But the main point is, you have more than 99% picked a wrong one, but put most of your assets in it. You will have a high chance of failure instead of being profitable. Don't fool by survivor's bias. Amazon lost more than 95% value of its stock price after the 2000 tech stock bubble, how can you know that it will become a superstar in the future.

How to observe for financial Fakery

Is there any big variance between the two financial years? This may be obvious when you are reading their financial statement. Except for some variance due to a change in financial standard or other observable reasons. For example, how can a firm significantly reduce its cost of production without any technologic advancement? How can a small market player in the industry have far higher sales per the same size than the top market leaders? Is it reasonable?

Do the statement of cash flow can't match with the company's strong sales for more than one financial year? Unreasonably high sales with high account receivable is a typical warning signal. I will state that checking for financial fakery is outside most of the individual investor 's ability. But we can keep some simple ideas in our mind, and don't put all your eggs in one basket.

A good company can be a bad investment

Understanding how good the company is operating is not enough, whether an investment is good also depends on the price of your purchase. A company with excellent performance can be a poor investment if it is overpriced.

If you purchase a stock which its price already "Price-in" the company's ten-year future growth, what else you can earn during those ten years?

I have seen many firms' stock prices traded more than 100years' future income in the emerging market. The company's stock price never can climb back at suck level even in the long run after the burst of a bubble. The market becomes a pure zero-sum game during a bubble, only depends who can be one of the very few winners in the game.

As an investor, we don't like suck kind of bubble market condition because we know that it is very harmful. Many of the new market players will become a loser, and it may also affect their families. We can't stop a bubble, and no market player will listen to your rational advice when they are seeing the stock price is moving up every day. They will blame you for disrupting them to win big money from the market.

We know, most of the money in their pocket will return to the market, but what else we can do…? Nothing we can do for others during a market bubble. For us, what we can do is don't purchase any additional stock when the market is in bubble stage, you can keep your original stock portfolio. A more conservative investor will consider reducing the risk exposure during the market bubble by selling some of the stocks. But this is a painful choice as the market is climbing up, you may lose some of the potential return when you are reducing your stock portfolio. What is appropriate depends on your risk preference.

Understand the nature of asset price bubbles.
Why we always consider the asset price bubble is harmful. All the price bubbles are a monetary phenomenon. Bubbles are mainly due to too many tracing limited assets.

Sometimes the investment object may be an asset that can be generating future income, and the investment object can be anything, such as a right to do something, a virtual item in digital formats. In real forms, it can be gold, jewellery, stamps, any commodity, such as the tulip fever happened in the 1630s. It can even be a stone you can find it a street, anything limited in supply can be used to trade, and create speculative bubbles,

The main point is, whether people believe that they have values? If the answer is yes, the next question is, do you people expected the price is going up in the future? If the answer is yes. Do most of the people join the game? If the answer is no, then the game can continue. If the answer is yes, the game will be ended very soon because the market players are not able to find new losers!

Most of the price bubbles are zero-sum games, one player 's gain is another player's loss. If the money is borrowed from the bank, one people 's gain may also be the bank's losses. If the bank loses too much, the bank will not be able to provide new credits to the public. If most of the banks have such a problem at the same time, this will lead to a credit crunch problem. Some people's gain in a speculative bubble will become society's losses, that's the case of the 2008 global financial crisis.

Understand the VIX Index and implied volatility

VIX index is considered as the Fear Index of the market, and it reflects the 30-days implied volatility of the S&P index. The idea is quite simple, of the index is 16, it means the market expected the annualized stock price most likely (around 67%) would be within +/-16% from the current price level, it means one month 's movement is very low.

The VIX index can be lower than 10, which means the market

consider the volatility is extremely low. This happened in 2017 to Jan 2018. The stock market was running a strong uptrend without any significant adjustment. This is because investors can easily purchase cheap insurance from the stock market. They do not need to take too much risk with their portfolio.

The VIX is not an index for price prediction. Many studies find that VIX sometime is a lagging indicator which means it follows the market trends. In my viewpoint, the VIX index can directly affect the market index instead of prediction. When the VIX index becomes lower, speculative investors such as hedge funds will find that investing in the stock market with option protection becomes a profitable option if the expected return of stock rebound is higher than the cost of hedging the long position of holding stocks portfolio. They will have the incentive to join back the market.

The VIX can sharply increase to above 40 in a short period during a sharp adjustment or market crash. If you look at the sharp adjustment in late 2018, you will find that, when the VIX index dropped off from its peak, the stock market can quickly form some supporting force. Now you know the mechanism behind the scenes. We all know the stock rebound in early 2019 is due to the

Fed changed its attitude toward the long-term interest rate, don't underestimate the join forces by the speculative purchase by the hedge funds. They will only gamble in any trades that they can have a statistical advantage.

Using Stock options as insurance for a stock portfolio
After you know about the basic idea of implied volatility. I would like to introduce a tool for active investors to manage the risk of their stock portfolio.

An option is rights that allow you to buy to sell the stock at a specific price within a certain period. The idea of using the stock option is very simple. For example, you can buy a stock option to protect your maximum loss to 10% in one year with a 1-2% (the actual cost depends on the market 's risk preferences) cost as stock insurance. This main disadvantage is you need to pay for around 1-2% of the total portfolio value to purchase that stock protection.

Buying insurance for something that is not at risk seems unreasonable. Therefore, the best time an investor considers using stock options is during the fanaticism stage of the stock boom. A typical signal is the market price is rising every day with very little adjustments.

At the final stage, the stock price will increase at accelerating speed. It is one of the best times to use stock options as the short-term insurance cost will be very lower, which professional investors will say that the volatility market is underpriced. Then your maximum loss of the period will be protected, you can sleep well, no need to worry about the market crash as your portfolio is now been protection by insurance at a low cost.

Example of using a stock option in trading
If the current a stock index ETF's market price at 300 USD.
You buy a one-year put option with a strike option priced as 18 USD. It means that your maximum loss of holding the stock portfolio is 18 USD as the put option will provide you with a right to sell the ETF at 300 before it is expired one year later. Your maximum loss is protected.

The above options implied volatility is around 16%, it means that the options market is expected that the stock index has around 67% of chance the stock index will be moving up or down within 16% of the current price level. The higher the implied volatility means the market has greater uncertainty, the insurance cost will be higher as well.

In contrast, when the market keeps on rising, the implied volatility of some medium-term option (maturity day within six months from now) may become very low, it means the insurance cost is very cheap. If you worry that the risk of the market crash becomes higher, you can consider buying some option protection that can hedge the downside risk instead of selling you portfolio which will lose all of the growth potentials in the boom phase.

We can buy option as an insurance for our stock portfolio, some traders can even sell options to earn extra return. But I must remind all the new investors never sell stock options unless you accumulated enough experience in the market. Selling naked option without hedging is one of the easiest ways to go bankrupt in the financial market. The discussion of further usage of stock options is outside the purpose of this book. Readers can refer to my recommended readings for further learning.

The Age of Negative Yields

The Age of Negative Yields

What are the negative yields?

Yield refers to the return of an asset. For stock investment, the yield comes from the stock dividend. For the bonds market, the yield comes from the coupon interest return of holding the bond plus the capital gain if the trading price of the bond is lower than its face value.

The yields become negative mainly happens in the bond market. It refers to a situation that the borrower will suffer capital losses if they hold the investment until maturity. Negative yielding bonds seems an unreasonable investment as no investor would like to invest in something that guarantees will lose profits.

How can an investor earn a positive return from trading a bond with negative yields? If the investor believes someone is willing to purchase the negative yield rate bond at a higher price, this transaction can generate positive returns. The buyer is the central bank which they can print money to buy those bonds with negative yields. Some Bond market traders can capture the yield changes for profits, and they don't care whether the yield rate is moving up or down, they can take advantage of different long and short positions. The market opportunity comes from price (/yield) changes, the positive yield is not a necessary condition for taking profit from the bond market.

The other way to earn a profit is from taking advantage of currency movement and from forwarding contracts. If you are an investor based on a country with a higher interest level, you can invest in other countries' negative-yielding bond with a forward contract that can lock the exchange rate with a positive return. That kind of idea is a bit difficult to understand, use a simplified example: if a government Bond of German is yielding at -0.2%, the US Yield rate is 1.5%, a US investor can earn a profit if the forward contract can earn an excess return (risk premium) if the net return is higher than 1.5%. Assume that the currency exchange rate 1US:1EURO, if the contract can let the US investor convert its Euro investment back to USD at a rate of 1.018USD per Euro after one year. Therefore, the return from the contract is 1.8%, after considering the negative bond yield. The US investor still can earn a little bit of excess return with such a diversified bond portfolio.

Some readers may ask why the bond fund manager doesn't directly hold Euro cash in the account (if the interest rate of the cash account is zero) instead of holding a bond with a negative yield. This is because many bond funds have investment restrictions which they are only allowed to investing certain types of bonds with very little proportion of cash. Another reason cash deposit in some country will charge for a negative interest rate as well. The benchmark interest in some currency already become negative (e.g. -0.8% EURO, -0.4 % Yen) in 2019. Holding bonds with a negative yield may perform better than holding cash balance in the bank account. You need to understand that financial institution who are holding too much cash will be punished in a country with a negative interest rate. Institutional investors need to invest in something to avoid being charged negative interest in the bank balance.

Besides, some bond investors may purchase certain bonds which can't generate expected profit. Some bond fund managers have limited investment choice for their investment portfolio. For example, a Japanese Bond Fund is unavoidable investing in some Japanese government bonds with negative yields. Individual investors can easily avoid such kind of financial bad holes, but some institutional investors can't, they are forced to buy some poor-performing assets.

What is the meaning of negative yields?
We come back to our main theme, what does negative yields

means for all of us. It is like a Dark Hole in the financial markets!

It will capture the investor 's long term returns in many markets. When you borrow money from some business institutions like banks, will it free of charge that doesn't have any interest. It seems impossible. However, this can happen in a market with negative bond yields.

A company will good creditability borrows $100 from the public, provides no coupon interest and will return the money to you five years later. The investors are willing to pay for $101 to purchase the bond right now. There aren't any typos. The investor is willing to pay you 101 today to obtain a right that can receive back $100 only five years later. Does it crazy enough? Negative yields are what happens in the financial market in some countries right now.

That kind of trade seems absolutely a loser 's game, and you must lose your capital when you hold the assets till maturity. Negative yields are like a dark hole that will destroy the investing capital. The borrower takes the money for free or even can generate positive returns, and the lender becomes a net loser.

Such kind of trade can be profitable for some party under a zero-sum viewpoint. If you know that a crazier buyer will be willing to buy your bond at 102, you can earn a profit by selling the bond with a negative yield.

The crazy buyer is the central bank, and they can print money to buy any assets at an unreasonable price. You can't understand this kind of practice by a traditional textbook, many of them are outdated in the new age. We need to review our old principle as many of them may not be appropriate in such a new age.

Understand our monetary system

In our modern monetary system, the money circulating is fiat money that is backup by the trust of the government only. The central bank as the agency of the government to manage the circulation of currency. If you look at the back of a US Dollar Note, you will find the word "In God we trust".

If the money supplied in the economy can easily be created, why people will be willing to use them for exchange goods and services. The value of the money comes from what you can buy with the money. The money can directly purchase for goods and service, and money can also purchase financial assets. Trillions of financial assets are denominated in USD, that's why most people trust that the US dollar has values.

The question is why the US and other developed countries created billions of money after the financial crisis. They lowered the interest rate to almost zero levels, and aggressively purchase the bonds to lower the long-term borrowing cost which is called quantitative easing. Their currency value doesn't have much depreciation pressure. Their inflation level remained at a very low level. It seems unreasonable.

Lesson from the history
In history, any small countries tried such kind of aggressive monetary policy will lead to hyperinflation and currency collapse. When a country quickly increases in money supply, it will lead to the inflation problem. If the country do not have strict capital control, the general public will have high incentive to exchange the domestic currency into foreign currency to maintain the purchasing power of saving, and this will lead to currency depreciation. The import product price may become very expensive and unaffordable for the locals.

If the country have straight capital control, the newly created money circulating in the economy will pull up the asset price level, people will try to buy any durable goods as quickly as they can. The general public will also purchase real assets or any portable jewellery instead of holding money. This may accelerate the inflation speed and leads to more serious hyperinflation problem.

When the economy is in deep trouble due to the collapse of the price mechanism, most of the country abandoned its original currency to save the economy. The country may issue some new currency with some valuable backups (like foreign currency or real assets) to replace the old one. Or the country may directly use foreign currency as legal tender.

Why the currencies' relative value still be stable?
As most of the developed countries lowering the interest together after the global financial crisis, the relative interest different between different countries is quite narrow. It means that if you print money yourself will lead to currency depreciation pressure, but all the countries print money together will not lead to currency depreciation.

Why there aren't any inflation problems?
This is another deeper question. If everyone has more money in their hands, all of them trying to buy more goods and services,

obviously, the inflation rate will be quite high. However, such kind of monetary inflation only benefits those who can borrow cheap credit from financial institutions, it means only a relatively small group of people can be benefited from such kind of monetary inflation. They get the jackpot, just open their bag to collect the money throwing out from the central bank. How? Leverage money to buy bonds and stocks, properties, any assets that can generate persistent positive yields.

The game will be ended if everyone becomes rich because it will lead to demand-pull inflation which the central bank will be inevitable to increase the interest rate, this may lead to another recession if the interest rate is raised too fast, we can see the trial evacuation exercise of the market in late 2018.

Another factor that will end the game is increasing in the wage level. Most of the public in the US do not have too much savings and assets that can benefit from asset inflation, but all the workforce can benefit from the wage rise. This will be the quickest way to burst the asset price bubble because once the wage level is rising quickly, the income will create demand pressure and speed up the inflation rate, the central bank has no options but using aggressive contractionary monetary policy.

The asset price bubble will burst instantly, or the central bank can choose "I kill you later". They ignore the risk of hyperinflation, let the inflation go. Look back at the case of the 1970s, this is one of the worst-performing periods for stock investors. The central bank will inevitable to raise the interest later, but with a sharper rate raise.

This case happened in Japan in the early 1990s, the Asset price bubble is burst, Stock market firsts, then the property market, then the whole economy. The lost decade is one of the worst-case that can be happened in a developed market. The GDP in terms of USD for Japan doesn't have any significant growth from the middle 1990s till now.

The bursting of a huge asset price bubble will not only harm investors, but this will also harm many innocents. The general public may face salary cut, unemployment increase, the new generation will become hopeless for growth, then declining birth rate, eventually reducing labor force and the growth potential due to the death cycle of declining population.

The government needs to raise taxes to support the welfare or keep on borrowing money. Japan's debts to GDP are more than 230%, but still increasing every year. This is a terrible cycle. It all started from an asset price bubble which is encouraged by the central bank in the middle 1980s. The central banks member most likely have a strong economics-related background, but lack of social and political sense, they always ignore their spillover effects to the society.

The different types of monetary policies?

You need to understand a different kind of monetary policies before you know what is happening right now.

The below are different types of typical monetary policy.

1) **Lowing interest rate**

    When the economy 's performance is not strong enough, the central bank may lower the short term targeted interest rate to encourage more credit consumption and investment.

    The central bank currently will also use forward guidance to influence the market 's expectation of future interest rate movement. This can help to encourage the firm 's long term investment plan if the forward guidance for the interest rate is lowering in the long run.

2) **Zero Interest rate**

   If the economic performance still not being good enough, the government will consider lowering the interest rate to zero or even negative. The business and consumption demand will not be increased too much by the lowering interest rate due to the liquidity trap problem, which means people and business already not sensitive to interest rate changes anymore.

   Most of the commercial bank will provide their depositors with a zero interest rate return for saving. They may even charge their clients with negative rates if they deposit too much when the bank has too much excess reserve which needs to be charged for a negative interest rate by the central bank.

   The lowest saving rate offer to depositor will be zero. Otherwise, people will consider saving their money in a home of a safety box in the bank. But this kind of practice will be very harmful to a bank's profitability as they need to pay for a cost for any excess reserve (idle cash). The bank may purchase some bonds with zero or even a negative rate to reduce the negative interest rate punishment from the central bank.

Zero lower bound

The investor should understand that the interest rate tools will become useless if the central bank reached the zero lower bound, it refers to an interest rate level that further lowering interest will have no positive effects on the economy. Besides liquidity trap, the impact of the interest rate policy also depends on capital outflow conditions. If a country lowers its interest rate at an extremely low level, investors will have incentives to move their capital to other countries to seek better returns. Such kind of capital outflow will create pressure on the exchange rate of the country, and it will also reduce the monetary base as the money is kept on outflowing to other countries.

U.S. central bank never allows the interest rate to touch the zero lower bound after the 2008 global financial crisis. The continuously lower interest rate may not also benefit the economy, it depends on the other country 's financial conditions. The zero lower bounds is not a constant level, it will also change over time if most of the developed countries' interest rate becomes negative. The zero lower bound for the U.S. economy in the future may become negative as well.

3) **Quantitative easing**

The central bank can also use quantitative easing to stimulate economic performance. They will purchase the long-term bonds, both government or corporate bonds in the second-hand bond market and release cash into the market. The reason for quantitative easing is the traditional interest rate policy mainly affect the short term money market condition, it may not affect the long term yield rate.

During the global financial crisis in October, although the short term interest rate is closed to 1% (and soon will become close to 0), the 30 years US government bond yield still at 4%. The long term corporate bond yield rate will be mostly higher than 4% as investors are required for a certain risk premium to invest in corporate bond (especially during a recession). Therefore, the U.S. central bank launched quantitative easing practice to lowing the long term borrowing cost for the economy.

When the bond yield of the government and corporate bond be lowered, the cost of borrowing of government and business will become lower as well. This can encourage more public expenditure and private sector investment. Lowering the long term interest rate can help to boost economic growth.

However, for some extreme cases, the central bank may even print money to buy a certain amount of stock market ETF and some other types of assets to support the asset price and indirectly support the economic growth. The Bank of Japan already started such kind of practice. The stock market will become harder to be crashed, as one big buyer is behind the market with the unlimited money supply. In theory, the central can use the money from quantitative easing to buy any asset they want, but the main concerns are the supply of assets have its limits. There are a limited amount of bonds or stock available for purchase, some European country's central bank always buying up most of the available bonds in the domestic bond market, and there is not much room left for using such policy to stimulate the economy in the future.

4) **Negative yields for long term borrowing**

How Negative yields works

If the long-term government bond 's yields become negative, the investor can earn a positive return when they are holding government bonds or investment-grade bonds.

Negative Yields can help to lower the firm 's cost of business. It also will create positive wealth effects that some people can earn profits from bonds trading.

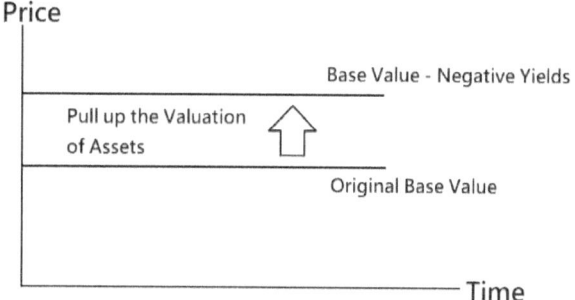

However, the effects of lowering interest may be short-lived. If the economic performance is not good enough, the need to further lowing the negative yields, let more investor benefited from the asset price increase. But this will have limits, the positive effects of negative-yields will be diminishing.

How Negative yields become Failure

Most of the assets already purchased by the central bank related agencies, there is little further room for asset purchase. People don't have the incentive to invest in any assets as all are an extremely high price. Many money becomes idle in the economy, and monetary policy will become useless to stimulate economic performance.

Actually, many newly printed money will outflow to other countries to seeking any positive yields. It cannot help to improve the domestic economy, the business and the general public cannot take advantage of such kind of aggressive monetary policy. Further lowering the interest rate only leads to financial distortion.

If the central do not able to normalize its interest rate during a boom cycle, it will have no monetary policy rooms to solve the recession problem during the recession phase.

Further asset purchase becomes impossible, and a huge asset price bubble accumulated in almost all major asset types. There is the main problem.

5) **Helicopter Money**

This is the final method of the central bank, and it works with the government fiscal policy together. The government can provide a basic income for the general public or using some indirect way like create more public sector jobs, social welfare to support the economy.

The idea seems not bad, but most of the historical cases will lead to hyperinflation as the government will heavily rely on printing money or issuing more debts. If the potential output of the economy can't support growth together, such a policy will lead to failure eventually. Look back at the European bond crisis in the year 2011, you will notice that without an ambitious government that can use the money to promote long term growth but support for short term welfare eventually will lead to serious problems.

The logic behind the monetary policy (Optional)
At the end of this chapter, I will talk about the ideas of the monetary model. This part may be too difficult for general investors which you can ignore them (as optional ideas).

The traditional viewpoint for money and the economy as below:

MV [Money Transacted] = PY [National Output]

M = Money Supply

V = Velocity of money

P = Price level

Y = Real Output

In the short run, we assume the Velocity of money is constant. Therefore, when the money supply [M] increase, the National output [PY] will be increased. The economy 's real output [Y] will be improved as well.

The idea is simple, more money circulating in the general public can lead to higher real output level as people will have a higher incentive to buy more goods and service.

In the long run, we will assume that the velocity of money (V) and real output (Y) is constant. In many of the academic researches, we find that such a simple model can explain many of the inflation level changes very well. If a country trying to save the economy by printing money only, the only result will be hyperinflation instead of long term economic growth. Economics growth should be caused by effective investment and growth of factors of productions. Printing money will not directly lead to economic growth.

However, if more money is circulating in the general public 's hand, and this leads to a higher level of consumption and investment activity. This kind of moderate monetary policy will have long term positive effects on real economic activity.

However, when a country considers adopting a more aggressive monetary policy such as monetary easing and negative yields, the increased money supply is not going to the output market, they may be only going to the financial market without any positive effects on the real economy.

The formula can be rewriting as below:
[Alpha Wong 's Theory of Money in a closed economy]

MV = PY + PaA
Pa=Price level of Assets
A= Financial and non-financial Assets

The increased in new money supply will mainly affecting the

financial and asset market only (PaA). This is what happened currently, the property market and stock market for many developed markets are at its highest level, but the real income of the general public does not have much improvement. Further injection of money into the economy mainly leads to further inequality of wealth instead of promoting economic growth.

In an open economy without capital account control. The actual model will be more likely as below:

[Alpha Wong 's Theory of Money in an open economy]
MV = PY + PaA + PfAf
Pf = Price level of foreign asset
Af= foreign financial and non-financial Assets

If the country continues to print money, it's bond market yields become negative, the stock market 's valuation becomes very high. Some of the new money will become hot money flow which will go to other countries' financial markets for seeking better returns.

The hot-money flow in some developed countries [PfAf] can eventually lead to a huge global asset price bubble due to such spillover effects!

Aggressive monetary policy will be very dangerous for the global economy, as all the asset market become extremely priced. The global economy does not have much real benefit from it. The real income of the general public doesn't change. However, the cost of living keeps on rising. The is because of the rental and some other living cost increased due to the asset price inflation.

Using increasing money supply to stimulate the economy is like drinking seawater when you feel thirsty. At first, it seems better, but you will become thirstier which can't solve the problem.

There are two main problem
1) Central need to continuously inject new money supply to the market to maintain the effect. Otherwise, the market interest rate will start to raise (lead to contractionary effects) after the central bank stopped its injection actions.

2) If the central inject 80billion per month, 12month later, the total money supply will be increased by 960billion. If the economy still can't recover to its full-employment level, the central bank may consider increasing the injection to 100billion per month. Each time when the central bank is increasing its total injection,

the additional positive effects on the economy will be diminishing. Until the market conditions can restore to normal, it may need a long way to go for normalization progress, or it will never be normal again similar to the case of Japan.

Explaining something with past reference is easy, projecting something never happened before is difficult, you should have an excellent understanding of how the market works. There are little hints of what will happen next if you type the word "negative yields" in the search engine. I will not mind sharing you with my views in this book, and such views are come from my previous learning for how the financial system works. But kindly remind that my prediction may go wrong, please judge it by yourself.

In the worst case, the young generation will not have any hope for their future as no matter how hard-working there are, and they are not able to build up any assets or even afford a small place for raising their family. They are barely surviving with their income, any little rise in direct or indirect tax or rise in the price of any necessity item like public transport fee, gas price etc. could lead to social chaos. The social tension will be increasing. It can lead to some extremely social and political conditions. it seems we are moving towards such kind of a world.

If most of the governments in this world notice the danger of such kind of toxic policy, hopefully, these conditions will never happen.

Inequality will become a big problem

Inequality will become a big challenge to the capitalist system during the age of negative yields. Ray Dalio states that the richest 1% of people 's asset is almost equal to the bottom 90%, we already in one of the age of the unequal world in terms of wealth and asset allocation. The solution is something that hard to be practiced in many countries - High Capital Gain tax and inheritance tax, with a certain level of transfer payment to the public.

Many may argue that this will remove the incentive to workers, but let us see what happened currently in France, in Chile, once some necessity raised price can lead to serious social chaos. What will happen if the world becomes more and more unequal due to the aggressive monetary policy in the future without fiscal policy to distribute the money from the handle of a small group of people to the general public.

The most peaceful case is, a party which suggests for higher capital gain tax will be in power, they will gradually change the tax and benefit system of your country. When populism and nationalism are rising all over the world, what are the non-peaceful case will be...?

Ray Dalio remind us to look back on what happened in the 1930s. I agree with him. Hopefully, this will not have happened if more people in power noticed such kind of dangerous problems, using their political wisdom and fiscal tools to rebalance the pressure inside the society.

An investor better be a good thinker
Some reader may argue why this stock investing book may have some irrelevant contents about social issues. If you are a serious investor, you should better be a thinker who should not just focus on the market itself. You should have some knowledge of politics, diplomacy, economics, and social issues.

If your country would like to tax you 90% of your capital gain, and they already have capital control that does not allow you to transfer your money unless you paid a once-off capital departure tax. Even you are the winner in the market. Eventually, you will become a loser.

A famous Japanese investor named Korekawa Ginzo, he owned 20 Billion Yen in early 1980, but he has been investigated and needed to pay for lots of tax due to his transactions and capital gains, he can't keep any of his assets and owed the 2billion yen tax payable from the government when he passed away. This story is not joking, this is some real things that happened before. That's why an investor should know something about the potential changes in their society. You should not ignore such kind of knowledge!

That's the reason why investors like Ray Dalio has a deep understanding of social and political changes, and this is relevant for investing. A government with a declining workforce and high level of national debts will have a high incentive to raise the taxes in all aspects.

A government with a growing workforce and raising tax revenue will have a higher incentive to reduce the tax rate, and liberalize its controls on the financial market, allowing more foreign capital to join with a more efficient system such as lower transaction fees and deregulations. They are allowing the foreign capital to join the market to create a bigger cake together, instead of some declining country trying to protect their small piece of cake. You will know which kind of country is more attractive for long term investors.

How to find positive returns in a distorted market.

For stock market investors, they can take advantage of the negative yields in the early stage. Negative yield is like an Inversed gravity force in the stock market, and it will keep the stock market 's valuation at a certain high level.

The valuation of the stocks market can keep at a very high level in a long period. This will increase the chance of a market bubble. In our traditional common sense, a market bubble must burst. Investors should notice that most of the bubble that burst quickly is financed by short term finance with a high-interest cost. No matter the sub-prime mortgage loans before 2008, or short-term leverage financial support the tech-bubble in the year 2000, or the 2007 emerging market boom in China and some other countries. Short term loans and hot money flow are the main fuel for the bubble. Therefore, what goes up must come down!

However, When the long-term borrowing cost becomes zero or even negative, the bubble can become bigger and bigger once more new credit is flowing in, and it can last for so long and can't burst easily because forced selling does not happen in the market.

If you are an investor that has long term capital, don't completely leave the stock market even during the bear market. At least keep your eyes on it.

Prepare certain idle cash for the worst case, recession, and bear market. The duration of the bad years will be quite short as the central bank will take a more active role than before, you will see a huge amount of money will flow into the financial market again after the next crisis.

Building up an investment portfolio in a bear market is an excellent opportunity for an investor. As we never know whether a bear market will happen again. You may not need to reduce your stock portfolio too much to avoid missing potential growth. Prepare some of your assets in long term government bonds, and as cash.

If any recession happened, your long-term bond 's value would be improved, and then you can switch some of them into the stock market, which is at a bargain price level. Then all you need to do is be patient, waiting for market recovery, and waiting for the valuation of the stock market into new heights.

If the recession didn't happen, your original stock portfolio still could earn positive returns, and your bonds will provide you with some stable cash flow and positive return as well. The above is a plan that can capture benefits from two different kinds of market situations.

Some investors may add 10% 's portfolio to Gold investment if they want to hedge the risk of monetary inflation. But the value of gold is unable to predict, and this may not be suitable for every investor. But if the market interest rate raises suddenly, this portfolio will suffer loss, you need to know any portfolio have their weakness.

As an individual investor, what can we do?
We are not able to prevent the asset price bubble by ourselves. We are not able to avoid the spillover effects from the recession either. What we can try to do is take advantage of it. If you are not able to save the world, at least save yourself first.

Recession will inevitably lead to declining in stock price, bond price, and other asset prices. We never know when the next recession will be happening? If you trust the inversed yield curve phenomenon, which the US economy will face a recession after the 3month US treasury bill rate is higher than the 10-year bond rate. It means the institutional investors expected the economy would have a high recession risk that they need to buy the long-term bonds to lock the long-term yield return instead of short-run interest. This already happened in March 2019. Based on the previous statistic, most likely the US economy may face another recession in the coming few years.

A rational investor should not always trust the past statistic, although this phenomenon has 100% accuracy in the past 50 years. We still can't explain why this simple yield curve signal can work so well. Is seems the market always smarter than the government.

The best attitude is, enjoy the best, prepare the worst. You need to rethink what will happen under the crisis, and what will happen after the next crisis.

The age of negative yields will become a long-term phenomenon after the next crisis. After the great sell-off during the crisis, any assets that can generate yield will become highly favorable for the new generation investors. The stock market will go through a V or W bottom and then come back to a new height. Why? Too much money will be tracing too few real assets in the new world.

History repeats itself again!

Know yourself

Before the end of this book, I would like to ask you a important question, do you know yourself? This is an important question for any investors.

What are your aims for investment?
If you invest for your retirement, which has more than a 20-year time horizon. You can increase the proportion of
higher risk asset such as stocks in your portfolio.

If your investment is for short-term capital gain, the return will be uncertain. This is because the short-term market return is unpredictable.

The annual average return for stock investment in the past is around 5 to 7%. If someone says that he can earn a 15% annual return persistently, most likely he is investing in a zero-sum game. If someone says that he can earn a 40% annual return persistently, the return is even higher than Warren Buffet in the golden ages, that one should be telling lies.

If you obtained a higher than 50% return in one year, don't be too excited. You may be entering a bubble market that will burst very soon, or you may be extremely lucky in a zero-sum game. That kind of return will not be persistent in the future. These are once-off return. Don't be fooled by randomness! Please understand that you may not always be that lucky in the long run. Change your investment method before you lose what you earned from the market.

What is your character?

Some "Braveheart" investors always loved to take high risk for their investment. They may leverage up their investment by borrowing, buying shares without liquidity, trading future and options for speculation. Trading those stocks which are sharply increasing, believe that trend following is one of the best strategies (when it is going up, it will be going up).

Sometimes they are right, sometimes they are wrong. Eventually, if they become overconfident by some consecutive succeed, a "Braveheart" investor most likely will make some fatal mistakes in the future, that mistake can take away most of the profits or even their investment principal.

Taking how much risks is a personal choice. If you are a risk-loving investor, I will recommend you build up some firewall that can protect your total assets. The idea is simple. You open a few trading accounts in different brokerage firms — each account trading different kinds of investment. If one account suffers a total loss, you still have the capital to continue the game. Otherwise, all your capital accumulation is like building a castle with sand.

For some investors that very worry about their investment return, I will recommend that they will only focus on long-term investment, and their investment risk should be reduced to an acceptable level. You can lower the risk by lowering the proportion of total assets into risky assets such as the stock market. If you only put 20% of assets in the stock market, even that market dropped 5% in one trading day, and you only suffer 1% in your total assets. Holding a comfortable portfolio means that you do not need always to update the stock price, you can eat well, sleep well when holding the portfolio.

Anxiety investors are a group of people that do not suitable for short-term investments. As they will keep on checking the price movement and fell badly when the price is going down. They will quickly sell their profitable shares when the price just increased a bit. If they believe that the stock market will grow in the long run and using some long-term investment scheme or monthly purchase for investing. They will feel more comfortable.

Impatience investor

An impatience investor is always joining the market as a trader instead of an investor. They love short-term trading, reading the books about Trend following, mindfully trading. Most likely they will love the book like ***The Reminiscences of a Stock Operator*** and ***Market Wizard Series.***

They are like an athlete in the campaign, trading for them is like playing sports, most likely that kind of trader will be retired at their 30s. Either they become rich enough that can quit the game, or they are poor enough which needs to join back the labor market.

The result is quite extreme, most of them will not be a winner, as one winner's profit in a zero-sum game is from hundreds of losers. This is a game that winners' take it all. For most of the public, never join such a game, unless you are enjoying the excitement more than your money.

Heartbreak trader

Heart Break trader is one of the worst types of people in the market. No matter they can take profit from the market, they are suffering in emotion. When they buy a stock, it is going up. They will regret why I didn't buy more before. When they sell their stock, they will look at the stock quotation, and once the stock price is going up, they will regret why do I sell it too early.

The painful and struggle will be increasing once the stock price going up further, the only way to save the trader is the market going down again or when the trader re-entre the position again.

Then the bad feeling cycle will be repeated after the trader entered a new position again. Once it is going down, they always need to consider whether to cut lose right now. Once it is going up, they always need to consider whether I need to buy more shares.

Their pain can finally be released when they don't have any position during a long holiday like Christmas. But they will entry such conditions again once they opened a new interested.
Don't be such kind of investor, no matter you are profitable or not, you are losing your happiness in your life!

Checklist before Investing

The important checklist before you are starting stock investment.

1) **Do you have long term capital?**

    Without long term capital that can be used for long years, you may be forced to sell the stock portfolio at a very low value.

    You should use your idle cash or saving which can be used as long term capital for stock investment. If your money has short term usage like university fees, down payment for buying a property, never put them in the market.

    Short term stock trading is a zero-sum game, you are gambling. If you win in one game, you can't stop for it, you will keep on seeking short term "opportunities" unless you lose big in a game later.

    Never gamble in the stock market, once you love gambling in the market, your fate is almost been known, it is not a matter of how it is the matter of when. If you don't have enough capital, the stock market is not a place for short term money, invest in your personal knowledge, enhance your working ability, improve your working income. Using your idle saving for long term investment in some core markets. This is the best way to improve your living standards.

2) **Do you have any borrowing?**
Leveraging can increase the return when the market moves in the same direction as you expected. However, once the stock market

3) **How much you can lose?**
If you want the stock continuously climbing up after buying, and the stock turns down after you sell. You do not understand how the market works.

The market will not always move in one direction, but with many times of fluctuations which is very hard to find where is going next. You may suffer some loss in during the trading period. If you are not well prepared for the possibility of the loss in the investment account. You have some hard feelings when you suffer loss, you would like to sell it for profit as soon as possible.

And you will even earn in big as you will always quit the position after a small level of stock adjustment. You will also feel extremely bad if your portfolio's value is declining during a stock adjustment or during a bear market. The market may find a new bottom, again and again. If you are not prepared for this kind of bad scenario, you may sell all your stocks at the worst time. It means you may sell it at the best time for long term investors to enter the market (at the bottom).

4) **Short term trading or Invest for the long run?**

Excepts for those day traders or market makers, if you don't have confidence your investment portfolio will generate long-run returns, never buy it or hold it for one single day.

Some investors may argue that they want to take medium-term profit for a short period. Yes, this may be profitable...But what happens if your position is trapped, the market keeps on decreasing, cut loss? Once you are trapped, you will have a strong feeling that wants to escape from the position to survive.

This is our human instinct, I was harm by such instinct so many times. Most likely you will be waiting and sell it at a price very close to your buying price. You seldom can profit from the market if it is not increasing in a straight direction.

You can earn little money during a bull market, lose money by repeating cut loss in a fluctuating market. Lose big money when the market is continuously down during a bear market because you will extremely struggle whether to quite the position and buy it at a lower price, or even more aggressively buy more at a lower price for a medium-term rebound to get back your money. Once you leverage your position, and the market is going down again, you will lose hugely. I hope that you no need to taste such kind of feeling.

5) **Do you have plans before investing?**
Planning before investing is a good practice. You can put all the worst condition in your plan, if something happen, what should I response.

For example, you may ask yourself whether you have the confidence to hold your position during a downturn? If you don't have such confidence, never enter a new position unless you have a good plan to manage such kind of risk. Once you entered into such kind of uncertain position, when the market going to an opposite direction against your prediction, you may consider selling it and repurchase it at a lower price later. You will certainly sell your portfolio when the stock market has any significant adjustment because you don't have the confidence to hold for it. You may be able to buy it at lower prices. But you are most likely not able to hold to position till it is highly profitable again. You will eventually sell it at another adjustment, and see the stock price suddenly raise, then you will wait and wait for another adjustment. But the adjustment may not come again. Once you have quit and buyback practice, you will certainly become losers in the market. You are either underperforming the market index or always cut loss and lead to capital losses.

If you have a good planning for investing an uncertainty item, an alternative approach is to separate your capital into several pieces. Only place a small proportion of your total capital in the market first to try an error. There will be two possible outcomes, your investment becomes profitable or you will be able to purchase more stocks at a lower price. Predict all the possible outcomes and prepare for it is a good practice for active investors.

If you are a passive investor, you only need to review the portfolio regularly and consider when to eventually quit the position for money. If you invest for your retirement, try to reduce the proportion of risky assets like stocks when you are closer to retirement age, especially take advantage of a bull market before your retirement.

6) **Do you know the market and yourself?**

Investors should know how the market works, some experienced investing already travelled through Bull and Bear markets, and they know how the market mechanism works. They also know when it will be failure soon. Even we are in the worst age, they know the spring will eventually come in the long term.

The most important difference is, they also know their own characteristic, they know their emotional response when the market going in the opposite direction. They will less likely to be harm by their irrational emotional and can identify the knowledge and the noise from the market. They know what they are doing.

Less experienced investors can create such a similar response and similar belief by learning and studying. Learning can shorten the progress to become a smart investor. But reading and learning itself is not enough to prove that you can be a smart investor. You need to be verified by the actual trading activities during a complete market cycle. If the market goes into another direction, you can comfort with it, and know what to do next. That's an important attitude for an investor to survive in the market for the long run.

If you don't know the feature of your investment portfolio, and you do not have enough confidence in its long-term performance. You can start your learning by buying a small portfolio first. Make sure the try an error cost is acceptable for you. Otherwise, you will run away from the market after several failure experiences and never come back again.

If you buy an investment portfolio based on a piece of good news, you may easily lose money by closing the position based on another updated bad news. You may become fooled by the news. If you have your own belief and understand the long-term potential of what you invest, you will not sell it even the market is moving down, because you know what will happen in the long run. Be patient is one of the most important characters for a long-term investor to be profitable from the market.

If you are interested in investment, it can be a lifelong game, we have 90 years old player in the market, such as Charles Munger. The market is always there, someone tells it is risky, someone tells it is good for everyone, whether it is good or bad, all depends on your own attitude for it. No one can force you to set up an investment position during the peak of the stock market bubble, right? The risk depends on greedy and fears inside your mind, it also depends on whether your understanding of the market.

Know the market, Know yourself!

Afterword

Afterword

Know yourself and know your enemy (the market), and you will never be defeated

- Sunzi's "The Art of War"

I paid huge tuition fees to Mr. Market to learn some of the ideas in this little book. This book is simple, but the logic behind is not that simple. Remind that think independently before you invest.

No investing related publications can be suitable for all markets. Some ideas in this book may no longer be appropriate in the future. That's why investment books are not a long-selling book type in the market. Most of the investor never read more than five books published before the 1980s, because most of the popular book will become outdated very soon and the return for the write is very little. A famous novel can sell for 1million copies, an investment book which can sell for 0.1million copies already be classics. Even the book written by some retired fund manager with a certain reputation, may not be able to sales for a few thousand copies. Therefore, seldom of them will have the incentive to write something.

As a writer and an educator, I want to try my effort to spread my knowledge to the public. If this book can help one more reader to better understand the stock market, it worth for all my efforts!

Ray Dalio states that we are at an age that our wealth distribution becomes highly uneven. I totally agree with him. When the age of negative yields eventually affecting the US, that kind of situation will even worsen. Savers will be punished, no more safe-haven assets, you can only choose to invest in neither overpriced bond market, negative return money market funds, any assets with stable positive yields are traded at extreme pricing.

Most of the public will not have such kind of knowledge and understanding about what will happen in that kind of distorted world. If your cost of borrowing is 0.5% only, you can earn profit by any investment that can generate a 1% return. If a corporation's cost of borrowing is -1%, you can earn profit by any investment that generates zero returns. They simply can issue bonds to earn. This is what I mentioned several times in this book - too much money is tracing too little real assets! The valuation of everything can become unreasonable, the financial world will be heavily distorted. Anyone who can borrow in bulk or issue negative yielding debts will be the ultimate winner in this distorted game.

In such kind of a world, the general public can be easily classified into two different groups, people who have assets and people who don't have assets. People don't have assets that need to be working day and night just for paying their basic bills and raise their children. People have assets just borrowing money and can earn even more. This may lead to serious social and political problems. Income and Capital Gain Tax reform or certain changes in government policy fiscal policy may become very aggressive. Even the rich, eventually may not be the winner due to social chaos or social reforms. This may become a loser's game, most of us become losers. Further discussion is a bit outside the propose of this investment book. Hopefully, that kind of situation will never have happened if the leaders know the side effects of some inappropriate policy.

At the end of this book, I would like to ask you an important question but don't have any answer provided:

What are your investment goals?

What is the goal of your life?

Your life goal will significantly affect your investment attitude.

Anyway, for most of us, the purpose for investing may be very simple – for a better life! For yourself, your family and your society. If you become successful, please think about what you can do to help with others, not everyone can become Bill Gates. However, if everyone moves a little step further to help others, our society will become far better. Our world will become winners benefits the all instead of winners' take it all.

If you like this little book after reading, don't forget to give a comment or recommend others for this book.

Thank you for your reading!

Appendix

Recommended Readings:

Classics for an Investor

Book Name	Author
The Intelligent Investor	Benjamin Graham
Common Stock for Uncommon Profit	Philip A. Fisher
A Random Walk Down Wall Street	Burton G. Malkiel
The Most Important Thing: Uncommon Sense for the Thoughtful Investor	Howard Marks

Classics for Trader

Book Name	Author
Reminiscences of a Stock Operator	Edwin Lefèvre
Market Wizard	Jack D. Schwager

Stock Selection

Book Name	Author
How to Make Money in Stocks	William J. O'Neil
Beating the Street	Peter Lynch

| The Little Book That Still Beats the Market | Joel Greenblatt |

Technical Analysis

Book Name	Author
Technical Analysis Explained	Martin J. Pring
Technical Analysis of the Financial Market	John J. Murphy

Asset Price Bubble

Book Name	Author
A Short History of Financial Euphoria	John Kenneth Galbraith

Mutual Fund

Book Name	Author
Common Sense on Mutual Funds	John C. Bogle

Asset Allocation

Book Name	Author

| The intelligence asset allocation | William J. Bernstein |

Stock Option

Book Name	Author
Options as a Strategic Investment	Lawrence G. McMillan

Business and Credit Cycle

Book Name	Author
Big Debt Crisis	Ray Dalio

www.ingramcontent.com/pod-product-compliance
Lightning Source LLC
Chambersburg PA
CBHW021402210526
45463CB00001B/198